SPIRITUAL DISCOVERY SERIES

BOOK STUDIES

HOW TO STUDY The BIBLE

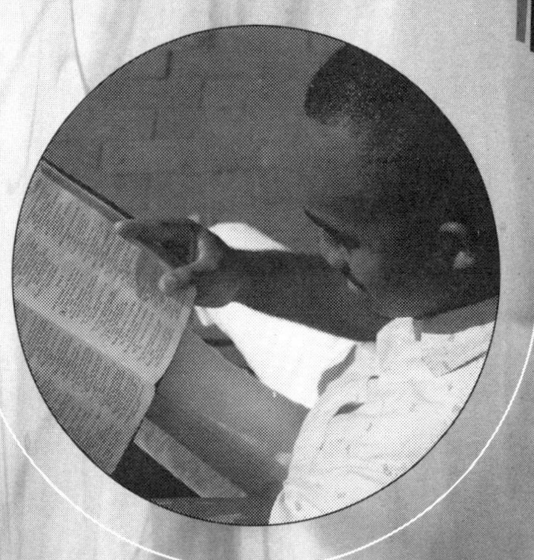

G. RAYMOND CARLSON

1445 Boonville Avenue
Springfield, MO 65802-1894
02-0108

STAFF

National Director: David J. Torgerson
Editor in Chief: Gary L. Leggett
Series Editor: Clancy P. Hayes
Assistant Editor: Lori Horne
Assistant Editor: Gerald Parks
Editorial Assistant: Terry Bryant
Design Director: Steve Lopez
Assistant Design Director: Marilyn Jansen

Photo Credits:
©1995 PhotoDisc, Inc.: Cover.; Mark Wright, Rockafellow Photography: Cover, 4, 15, 49, 78, 88; Gail Denham: 60; Fine Image Photography: 31; Donna Meier: 39; Norhill Photography: 7; Skjold Photographs: 70; Jim Whitmer Photography: 23.

Springfield, Missouri 65802-1894

Library Of Congress Catalog Card Number 95-78051
International Standard Book Number 0-88243-108-0
Printed in the United States of America

A Leader's Guide for individual or group study with this book is available (order number 02-0208). ISBN: 0-88243-208-7

Contents

Welcome To The Spiritual *Discovery* Series

We are glad you have chosen to study with us. We believe the discoveries you make through the use of the *Spiritual Discovery Series* will positively impact your life.

The *Spiritual Discovery Series* will challenge the user to ask questions of the biblical text, discover principles from the text, and make personal application of those truths. The Bible is the text. This guide is a tool for study.

The *Spiritual Discovery Series* is designed for use in either individual or group settings. Individuals will be excited by the discoveries made possible through a structured inductive study. Sunday School classes and other groups will find the *Spiritual Discovery Series* a valuable tool for promoting enlightened discussions centered on biblical truth.

How To Use This Study Guide

1 **Pray before beginning each study session.** Ask the Holy Spirit to illuminate your mind.

2 **Choose a translation of the Bible which you trust and can understand.** It will be helpful to have more than one translation available to aid your understanding of the biblical text.

3 **The Bible is your primary text.** Avoid using commentaries or reference books until after completing your own study. Reference works are best used to confirm your findings. On occasion, the study guide will direct you to use reference material. This is done when special insights are necessary for proper interpretation.

4 **Read the assigned biblical text at least twice before answering any questions.** This will provide an overview and focus on God's Word.

5 **Concentrate on the biblical passage which you are studying.** It is tempting to jump from one passage of Scripture to another in an attempt to make spiritual connections.

6 **Seek tangible ways to apply the principles gleaned from each study.** Bible study should never result in "head knowledge" alone. Bible study should lead to action.

Study 1

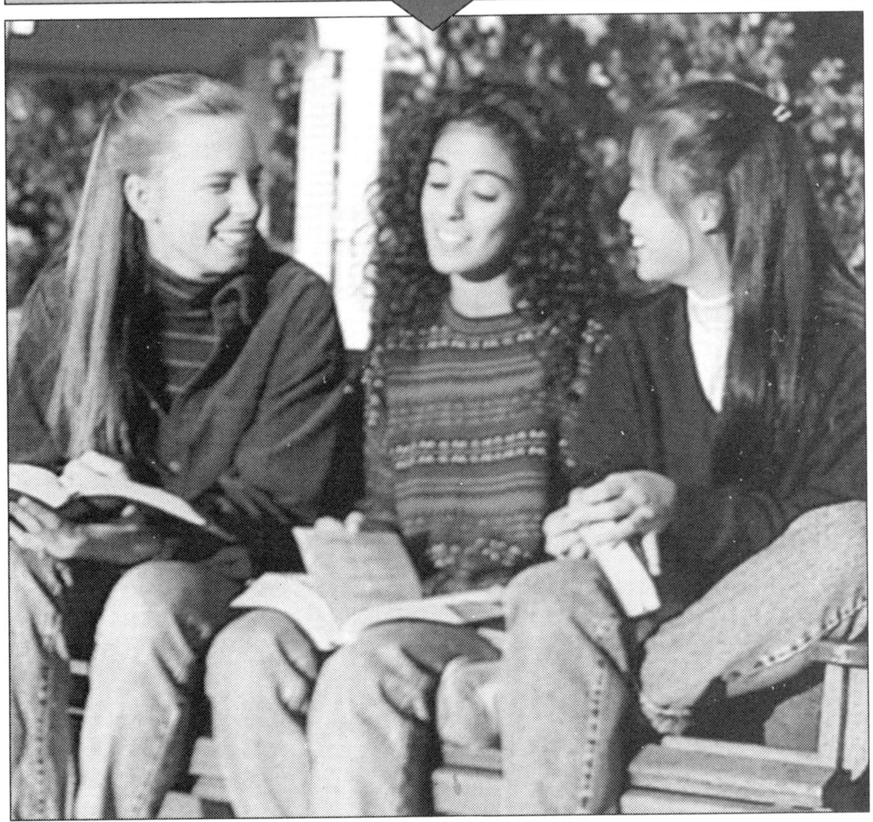

Why Study The Bible?

Every Christian should and can know his Bible. Bible study is not optional for the Christian. Some may object that they have neither the skill nor the time to study the Scriptures.

During the next few weeks, several studies will expose individuals to principles and methods of Bible study. The decision to establish a regular time and place for Bible study, however, rests squarely with the individual.

It is important that each Christian understand the need for, and then make a commitment to, personal Bible study. This study will explore biblical passages which provide the rationale for consistent, systematic Bible study.

Depth Of Understanding

Read Acts 17:10,11

The people of Berea have long been examples to Christians for Bible study. Churches, Bible classes, and clubs have been named for the studious people of Berea. The Bereans were an example of real nobility in Christian living, for they searched the Scriptures daily.

1. Acts 17:11 compares the Bereans to the people of Thessalonica. How does Paul describe the Bereans' character?

____

The word *noble* usually refers to men of the aristocracy, men of noble birth. In this instance the reference is to noble character.

God delights in people who love His Word, people who respond to the preaching of the Word. Anointed listening and anointed preaching are both needed.

2. According to Acts 17:11, what did the Bereans do to verify the truth of Paul's words?

____

3. What does this teach us concerning our obligation as we listen to a person proclaim God's Word?

____

____

4. What is the danger of listening to a sermon, but not following the Bereans' example?

____

____

5. As important as Bible study is, it is not an end in itself. According to John 5:39,40, what is the ultimate purpose of Bible study?

____

____

Some people search the Bible with a skeptical, even an antagonistic attitude. Their search is not noble. The noble seek for comprehension that is clear, for understanding that is intelligent.

Inquiry will be rewarded if we come with a humble heart and prayerful spirit. The Holy Spirit stands ready to reveal truth to us if our inquiry brings us to the Scriptures and the searching of God's revealed Word. If we search in this manner, we too shall receive. True followers of Christ are students of the Bible who are always searching and receiving.

FOUNDATION FOR LIVING

Read 2 Timothy 3:14-17

The Word of God is sure and dependable. It is "God-breathed." Blessed are those who, like Timothy, have had the precious and powerful influence of the Word on them from childhood, and who in their mature years continue to live by the principles they have learned.

6. Compare 1 Timothy 4:16 with 2 Timothy 2:14. What is the emphasis in these verses?

____

What Timothy had learned in childhood (2 Timothy 1:5) had now been made real by experience. He was to pursue obediently the very same truths that he had already received, neither adding to nor taking away from them.

Timothy had learned his doctrine from Paul (2 Timothy 3:10) but he was reminded that he had been raised on the Word of God. It may have been that his mother and grandmother combined their efforts to make up to Timothy for his lack of a godly father.

Youth is the best time of life to receive truth and to give one's life in service to God. While each person's salvation is a personal matter, the value of godly parents cannot be overestimated. The more harmonious their lives are with God, the greater will be their influence on their children. It is the duty of Christian parents to lay a foundation for their children that will fortify them against evil.

Timothy received training and assurance in the Word of God. That Word came from the Holy God through holy men who were inspired by the Holy Spirit. The Holy Spirit, who breathed inspiration into the pages of Holy Writ, breathes illumination to us.

7. Use a standard dictionary and record the primary definition of the word *illumination.*

____

____

8. Why is the Holy Spirit's illumination important to those who wish to study the Bible?

____

____

 **9. What two facts does Paul declare about the Scriptures in 2 Timothy 3:16?**

The inspiration and authority of Scripture will be explored in detail in our next study. But we must start with the truth that the Bible is God's Word to man. As such, it is vital that Christians make the effort to understand and internalize its truth.

In 2 Timothy 3:16,17, Paul declares that as people of God, with a thorough knowledge of the Bible and with the blessing of God, we will be equipped for every work to which He calls us. We read the Bible to see how people should live. The Word and the Spirit will produce in us a godly life through obedience.

LIFE OF DISCIPLINE

Read 2 Timothy 2:15

This verse does not primarily refer to studying. The old English meaning of *study* is "to be diligent." Rendered "study" in the King James Version, it is "be diligent" in the New King James Version and "do your best" in the New International Version. For us to be diligent in holding a straight course in the Word of truth will require our best study. God calls us to a diligent presentation of self to Him for His approval. That approval comes to those who have a thorough grasp of His Word and handle it correctly.

The word translated "approved" is one which is used almost exclusively by Paul in the New Testament. It connotes ceaseless, serious, earnest zeal, a characteristic of the apostle.

 **10. According to 2 Timothy 2:15, what is approval based on in this circumstance?**

Every workman should attempt to be the best possible worker in his craft. This should be preeminent in the thinking of the Christian worker. A Christian is to be approved by God, unashamed before God, and unashamed before fellow workers. This requires diligence in preparation and in service.

 **11. According to 2 Timothy 2:15, what is the result of being approved by God?**

The phrase "rightly dividing" literally means, "cutting straight." It has also been defined as "holding a straight course." The expression is derived from various sources. Some believe the figure comes from a priest dividing the sacrificial animal, or the carpenter or the stonemason cutting straight lines. It is a term used for the plowman making a straight furrow, or the road builder laying out a straight road. The latter was a characteristic of Roman roads. Paul and Timothy would be familiar with this. No doubt the apostle used the phrase, "cutting a straight course," when plying his trade, cutting out the material to make tents.

Paul urged Timothy to be straightforward in his handling of the Word. The teacher must lay down a straight and true way for the listeners through the teaching of the Word. The Bible must be handled properly to give its true meaning and application.

12. Paul gave a positive directive to Timothy in 2 Timothy 2:15. Paul approached the same subject from a different angle in 2 Corinthians 4:2. Paraphrase 2 Corinthians 4:2 below.

____

____

____

____

____

13. Christians have been commissioned to share the gospel with others. How can we be assured that we will not fall into the category of false minister or teacher as we communicate truth to others?

____

____

____

TRANSFORMATION OF CHARACTER

Read Hebrews 4:12

Read the broader context of Hebrews 4:12. Note the connection with the preceding portion of Scripture. The writer of Hebrews urges us to be cautious of unbelief and presumption, of doubting and indifference, for God's observations are keen; His testings are exact and searching. The seriousness that should control our thoughts, our faith, and our actions is the realization that our bodies, souls, and spirits are under two searching critics—the Word of God (Hebrews 4:12) and the eye of God (Hebrews 4:13).

14. Hebrews 4:12 describes the Word of God in four ways. List the four ways below.

____

____

The Bible is the living Word, possessing life as Christ the Living Word claimed for himself (John 14:6). The Word is not a dead letter, but is full of life.

15. Describe a specific time when the words of the Bible became alive and personally spoke to you.

____

The Word is also "powerful." Another translation is "active" or "effectual." It is powerful in its effects and able to accomplish the purpose for which it is sent forth.

16. One of the most powerful ways Scripture expresses itself is through changed lives. Relate an event that you have experienced or witnessed where the Word of God transformed a person's life.

The sharpness of the Word is yet another feature. It penetrates even to dividing soul and spirit. As a two-edged sword, it cuts into the innermost recesses of a man's life. The Word, accompanied by the Holy Spirit, exposes the evils of the soul and spirit. Paul declares the Word is "the sword of the Spirit" (Ephesians 6:17); John presents Christ, out of whose mouth "went a sharp two-edged sword" (Revelation 1:16; compare 19:15). Jesus was—and still is—a divider of men (John 7:51-53); His Word also divides.

A sword in the hand of a veteran of combat is effective. With it he can parry and feint, jab, slice, and stab. The Word operates on the human heart in this manner. But it is more devastating than any sword because it is sharper. A sword divides flesh, severs arteries, and cuts through bones; the Word cuts into the spiritual life and cuts through the joints and marrow of the inner life.

The Bible is also discerning, literally the "critic" or "judge" of the very thoughts and intents of a man's heart. This is good news for the believer, but awful for the unbeliever. The written Word, as the Living Word did when on earth, penetrates into the corrupt depths of the heart. The written Word of God, when focused in full force upon a person, will pierce to the depths of his being and expose him for what he is.

17. Some consider God's judgment a dreadful experience. This need not be the case. What is the correct response to God's judgment against sin in our life? (Acts 3:19).

MANDATE FROM GOD

Read 1 Timothy 4:13-16

18. There are four commands made in 1 Timothy 4:13-16. List the four below.

____

____

____

____

Timothy had a godly heritage handed down from his mother and his grandmother. But he did not coast along on the impetus of a Christian home. He read and taught as he had been taught. With diligence he used the gifts God had given to him.

There is no easy road to learning. Every effort must be put forth to draw from the Word of God. The truth that is learned must first be applied to ourselves, and then passed on to others. There is no place here for the lazy person. Preparation of heart and mind will enable us to lay hold of the Word to save ourselves and those who hear us.

There are two Greek words which are almost alike, used in 1 Timothy 4:13-16. The first (verse 13) is translated "give attendance" or "devote yourself"; the other (verse 16) is rendered "take heed" or "persevere." The first means "to have before you," the last "to have upon." Timothy was urged in the first instance to have the reading (Scriptures) "before him" for study at all times. In the second instance he was "to have upon himself" the doctrine, to apply what he read to his own life. It is one thing to read words; it is another thing to apply the words to our lives.

SUMMARY

There are a variety of practical reasons for studying God's Word. Bible study provides a depth of understanding, a foundation for living, a life of discipline, and when heeded, a transformation of character. Most importantly, Christians have received a mandate from God to grow through the study of His Word.

An understanding of the rationale for Bible study does little good if the individual Christian does not set aside specific blocks of time to actually study God's Word. It is essential to a Christian's spiritual health to make a habit of Bible study. In order to do this, one must make a commitment to study on a daily basis. Each of us find time for those things we consider important. Personal Bible study must be seen as a priority if it is to become a reality.

Bible study is hard work which pays long-term dividends. Will you commit yourself to a regular time of study beginning today?

LET'S REVIEW

1. Why were the Bereans considered noble?

2. What does 2 Timothy 2:15 mean? Hebrews 4:12?

3. What is meant by "rightly dividing the word of truth"?

4. What are the benefits of consistent Bible study?

5. What steps can one take to create the habit of personal Bible study?

Study 2

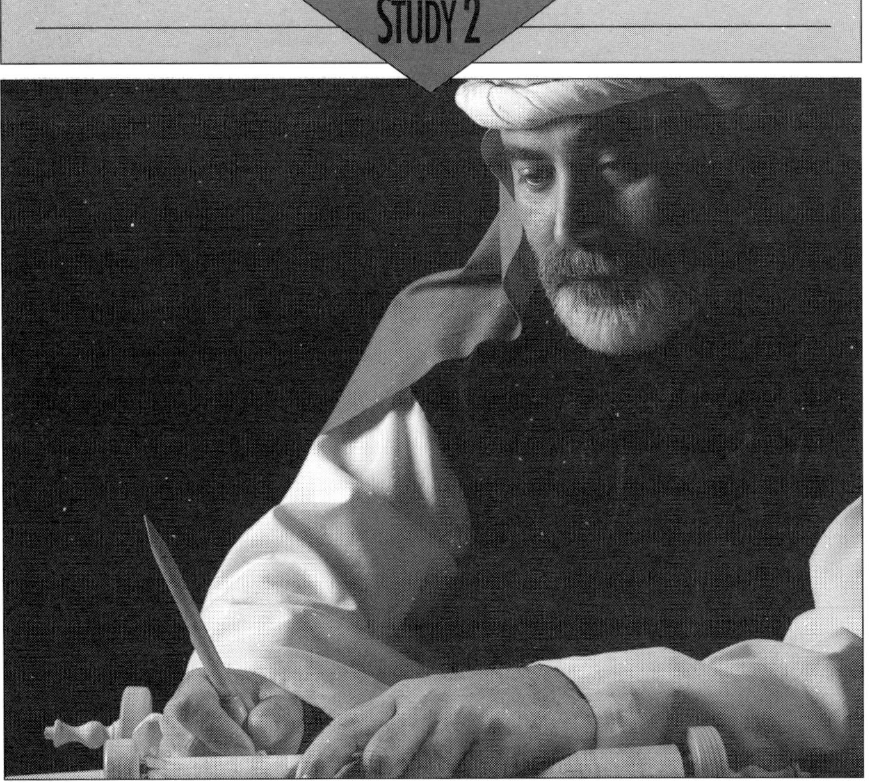

The Authority Of God's Word

The Old and New Testaments form a collection of 66 distinct books. These books were written in at least 3 languages by about 40 different authors, during a period of about 1,600 years. Each book is a literary whole, and at the same time each is a part of the larger whole, making its own distinctive contribution to the revelation of God.

The Bible is an unfolding of God's truth to man which leads man to God and provides a basis of fellowship with Him. Biblical Christianity is the revelation of God; it is not a man-made faith arrived at by the faulty guesses of men. The 66 books of Scripture—no more, no less—is God's complete message to us. The Bible alone is the Word of God. Evangelicals insist on two things about the Bible—that it is divinely inspired and that it has absolute authority in all matters of faith and practice.

THE BIBLE: GIVEN BY GOD

The Bible is the most remarkable volume ever produced in the some 5,000 years of writing by the human race. On this fact men must agree despite what they may think of the message and authority of the Book. The Bible stands above all other literature as to content, circulation, and influence.

The Bible is an infallibly inspired Book, given by God to man for his edification, guidance, and blessing. This is a foundational belief of Christianity. Christianity stands or falls with the truth or falsehood of the Bible.

1. Turn to 2 Timothy 3:16,17. Write the passage in the space below.

____

____

2. Summarize 2 Timothy 3:16,17 in your own words.

____

____

3. The Bible is viewed in many ways. Some see it as literally God's word to man. Others view it as a good book. Yet others view it as outdated folklore. What do you think?

____

____

If the Bible is only the work of men, we can never lean on it for spiritual support. If it is no more than a human work, it must be a mere compilation of the ideas of man about ethics and morality, interwoven with a record of Jewish history. But the Bible is more than the work of man; it is inspired of God.

What is inspiration? Inspiration is a special act of the Holy Spirit by which He guided the writers of Scripture, making sure that their words were free from error and omission and that they conveyed the thoughts which the Holy Spirit desired.

The word *inspired* comes from the Latin and means "inbreathed." The Greek word *theopneustos* combines God and breath. *Theos* means "God" and *pneuma* means "breath." These two words combine in the Bible to make *theopneustos*, which is translated "inspired by God" or "God-breathed."

The inspiration of the Bible means its contents were communicated to the writers by the Holy Spirit. That which is inspired is God's Word—written by human hands, molded in some degree by human thought, and using human words. Under the influence of the Holy Spirit, the writers were prevented from writing anything but what God intended. God so controlled the writer that the words written were exact and correct.

Evangelicals in all parts of the world are united on the doctrine of the inspiration of the Holy Scriptures. However, there is an amazing divergence of opinion today about what is meant by inspiration. New ideas have appeared on this important tenet of the faith. But if there is one truth on which Christians must be firmly established, it is the doctrine of the inspiration of the Holy Scriptures. We must be clear as to the method of inspiration as well as the fact of inspiration.

4. Why is belief in the inspiration of the Bible such a central issue?

____

____

5. How would the Christian faith be different if the Bible were not inspired?

____

____

VERBAL PLENARY INSPIRATION

What is meant by verbal inspiration? Verbal inspiration means every word in the original manuscripts was inspired by God. This does not mean, however, that the writers were mere secretaries who took dictation from the Almighty. The writers were not robots. Each Bible writer used words in his vocabulary which the Holy Spirit approved and prompted him to use. In some cases this was direct dictation, as with Moses, who wrote exactly what God gave him. In other cases it was less direct, but no less exact. Scripture passages supporting verbal inspiration include 1 Thessalonians 2:13; 2 Timothy 3:16; 1 Corinthians 2:7-13; 11:23; 14:37; Galatians 1:11,12,16,20; Ephesians 3:1-10; 2 Peter 1:19-21; 3:15,16.

God used about 40 men to write the 66 books of the Bible. No two were alike, but God used the vocabularies, styles, and personalities of each writer to record His exact revelation. In other words, the human authorship was respected to the extent that the characteristics of the writers were preserved and their styles and vocabularies were employed without error. This involved a mysterious interaction between the Spirit of God and man.

What is meant by plenary inspiration? By this we mean full inspiration of all Scripture as against partial inspiration. Verbal inspiration brings an accuracy that insures full inspiration for every portion of the Bible. To sum it up: the whole Bible is God's Word written by men.

In today's society, we are used to going to the grocery store and being able to pick from a variety of items. Some things we like and purchase. Other things we leave behind. The Bible is not like a supermarket. You must take it all or have none.

6. What are some areas of the Bible that you have neglected? What must you do to remedy this?

____

____

The historic doctrine of the verbal plenary inspiration of the Bible is under grave attack today. The Christian need not base his defense of this vitally important doctrine upon the fact that it is historic. The doctrine must be defended because the Lord Jesus Christ and the Bible itself demand it. (See Luke 10:26; Romans 4:3; Galatians 4:30; Deuteronomy 31:16-19; Psalm 9:7-11; 2 Samuel 23:2; Galatians 1:12; 2 Peter 1:20,21.)

THE BIBLE CAN BE TRUSTED

7. Read John 10:35 and 1 Thessalonians 2:13 and record your insights below.

The Word of God is complete. It needs no additions and tolerates no subtractions. The Bible is an authoritative Book having authority to control our actions and to give us an answer to life's questions. It is the infallible, authoritative rule of faith and conduct.

The words *inerrancy* and *infallibility* need explanation. *Inerrant* means the state of being free from error. *Infallible* means incapable of error.

The Word of God is infallible because God himself is infallible. What the Bible says is to be received as the infallible Word of the infallible God. To believe in the inerrancy and infallibility of the Scriptures is to believe that they are of divine authorship and that God and His Word can be totally relied upon.

8. The statement that the Bible is without error and cannot fail provides security. Cite specific scriptural truths which have given you strength in troublesome times.

The infallibility of the Bible applies to the original manuscripts, not translations and versions. Competent scholars have brought our English versions to a remarkable degree of accuracy, however, and we can rest with confidence upon them as authoritative. For the Christian, the Bible is the supreme court from which there is no appeal.

9. There are differences in the various translations and versions of the Bible. Look through a variety of Bibles and note the differences in language. Why might these differences exist?

How We Received Our Bible

Not all the writings of Jews and Christians became a part of our present-day Bible. Those that did are said to be "canonical" and are deemed the authoritative Scriptures of the Church. The process by which certain writings became a part of our Bible is called "canonization." Those writings that were rejected are said to be "apocryphal" and are called the Apocrypha. The word *apocryphal* means "hidden" and may have reference to the difficult nature of its content.

The Old Testament Apocrypha is comprised of 13-15 books, depending on which grouping scholars choose to make. While these books are used by various groups of Jews and Christians, a long line of evidence from antiquity (both Jewish and Christian) stands against accepting these works as canonical.

The formation of the Old Testament canon, made up of the Law (*Torah*), the Prophets (*Nebim*) and the Writings (*Kethubim*), took place over a long period of time. Historians know little about how Jews came to recognize these works as the Word of God. The meeting of Jewish scholars at Jamnia around A.D. 90 rejected the Apocrypha and gave official recognition to the 39 Old Testament books we find in our Protestant Bible.

Jesus told His disciples that all things written about Him "in the Law of Moses, the Prophets, and the Psalms" must be fulfilled (Luke 24:44, NIV). The criteria used by Jews in judging and accepting the books of the Old Testament canon are not specified in any ancient document. Nevertheless, it is most probable that the tests of canonicity included questions about the origin, character, and effect of the writing.

While the writings of the New Testament belong to the first century, the formation and recognition of those writings as a canon of Scripture called the New Testament took place over the next three centuries. The Church during that time was presented with many texts as candidates for the New Testament canon. Some (called *Homologoumena*) were immediately accepted by nearly the entire Church. Others (called *Antilegomena*) were disputed for some time by parts of the Church, but later accepted as canonical (Hebrews, James, 2 Peter, 2 and 3 John, and Revelation). A large number of books (called *Pseudepigrapha*) were almost universally rejected. Still others were recognized for a time by some but were later dropped from canonical lists. Eventually most of the Church came to a consensus regarding the contents of the New Testament.

New Testament scholars speak about the "closing" of the New Testament canon. This refers to the Church's restricting the contents of the New Testament by listing the writings which alone were to be regarded as authoritative Scripture.

The earliest manuscripts of the New Testament were written in Greek. It was not until the 14th century that the Bible was translated into English. Since then numerous English versions have been developed.

The Wycliffe Bible (1384)

John Wycliffe (1330-1384), a freethinking Oxford theologian, felt that each man was immediately responsible to God and accountable to His law, which he equated not with Church law, but with the Bible. He felt a great burden to see the whole Bible translated into English. In 1382 his teachings were branded heretical. He was forced to retire to his rectory and died 18 months later. The Wycliffe (or Wyclif) Bible was produced between 1380 and 1384 by Wycliffe's friends and colleagues who were inspired by his views and example. As a translation, it is an extremely literal rendering of the Latin Vulgate, sacrificing English idiom to preserve the Latin word order.

The Tyndale Bible (1525)

William Tyndale (1494-1536) had a passion to see the Scriptures translated into the mother tongue of all people so that they might understand them. An Oxford scholar, he possessed excellent translation skills and later studied at Cambridge where a "new learning" stressed the study of Greek and Hebrew biblical manuscripts. Tyndale wanted to produce a translation of the Scriptures based on those manuscripts rather than Latin. Such an endeavor was unlawful without episcopal approval and Tyndale could secure none. In the home of a friend, he translated most of the New Testament. In 1524 he sailed for the European continent, completing the project in 1525.

Appearance of his English New Testament in England incurred the wrath of the Bishop of London who initiated a burning ban of Tyndale's work. Despite being continually harassed, Tyndale completed his translation of the Pentateuch in 1530 and a revised edition of his New Testament in 1534. Treacherously betrayed in 1534, he was imprisoned. Tyndale was burned at the stake in 1536 but not before he had translated most of the Old Testament.

The Coverdale Bible (1535)

Myles Coverdale (1488-1569) is credited with publishing the first complete Bible in English in 1535. He knew little or no Greek or Hebrew. His work was based on Luther's German translation, Tyndale's English translation, the Latin Vulgate, and two other translations. His Bible was the first to separate the Apocrypha from the canonical books.

The Geneva Bible (1560)

During the persecution of Protestants in England under Queen Mary, many English Protestants fled. William Whittingham, a competent scholar in Greek and Hebrew, who lived in Geneva, completed a preliminary revision of Tyndale's New Testament in 1557. In 1560 he finished a translation of the entire Bible based on Greek and Hebrew manuscripts in consultation with a number of foreign language translations. The Geneva Bible became extremely popular and its extensive annotation did much to spread Reformation doctrine.

The Douai Bible (1610)

William Allen sought to reconvert England to Roman Catholicism by means of an English Bible promoting Rome's teaching. The New Testament was published at Rheims in 1582 and the Old Testament at Douai in 1609 and again in 1610. Translated from the Vulgate, it tried to literally reproduce the Latin text. The result was an inferior translation, rigidly literal without good English idiom.

The King James Version (1611)

After the death of Elizabeth, James I summoned a conference of clergy and scholars in January 1604. The conference resolved to translate the Bible from the Hebrew and Greek. This translation was to be void of sectarian notes and to be used in all the churches of England. Six teams divided up the work of translating the Old Testament, New Testament, and the Apocrypha. Each team's work was reviewed by a group composed of two people from each team. Completed in 1611, the Authorized Version or King James Version (KJV), as it is called today, was without question the most carefully researched, responsibly conducted translation of the Bible into English up to that time. It has undergone numerous revisions; the most significant change was the permanent omission of the Apocrypha in 1826.

Present-Day Versions

While the King James Version has been the most popular and widely read English Bible for more than 350 years, numerous English Bible translations have been published. Some of the more popular versions are as follows:

1. The New American Standard Bible (NASB) first appeared in 1971. It was produced by 54 conservative scholars. The goal was to provide an accurate translation that closely followed the word order of the Greek and Hebrew texts. Many consider it the most literal translation.
2. The New International Version (NIV) was completed by 115 evangelical scholars in 1978. Its purpose was to produce a translation in contemporary English that retained the traditional biblical vocabulary. Its sensitivity to conventional English usage has made it a most popular and readable version.
3. The New King James Version (NKJV), completed in 1982, was the work of 119 scholars. It represents a conscious effort to modernize the wording of the KJV. It also attempts to represent the content of the Greek and Hebrew manuscripts on which the KJV was based, and not those of earlier texts discovered after the publication of the KJV.
4. Today's English Version (TEV or Good News Bible, 1976) is the translation of Robert Bratcher and six other scholars. This version attempts to produce an easy-to-read, free-flowing, English translation of the original texts. It seeks to avoid traditional biblical vocabulary by replacing it with conceptually equivalent words or phrases.

SUMMARY

It is obvious that God has superintended the transmission of His Word through the ages. We can rejoice that God has made the Bible available to us in our own language so we can be saved and find God's will for our lives.

But how does one evaluate the numerous versions of the Bible available today? Part of the answer depends, of course, on what you are looking for. Almost everyone wants an "accurate" and "readable" translation in the Bible of his or her choice. But what constitutes accuracy? Literalness may or may not be accurate. Free translations may be readable, but are they always accurate? It seems that the good translation must be understandable. It must communicate the words of the biblical text not only in equivalent English terms, but in terms that convey the meaning intended by the biblical writer.

One other consideration in choosing a Bible version should be mentioned—utility. This surely incorporates the other qualities of a good translation and is, in one sense, a by-product of them. Utility addresses the usefulness of a particular translation to bring about a personal hearing of the Word of God in one's life, resulting in salvation, spiritual growth, and maturity.

LET'S REVIEW

1. What is meant by inspiration?

2. What is meant by inerrancy and infallibility?

3. What is the canon of Scripture?

4. Briefly summarize how we received our English Bible.

5. How does belief in the inspiration, inerrancy, and infallibility of the Scriptures give us confidence to rely on the Bible to guide us in our daily living?

Study 3

Tools For Bible Study

The most important book to use in the study of the Bible is the Bible itself. Too many people read a lot of books about the Bible but read the Bible itself very little. True Bible study must begin with the Book, for the Bible itself is primary.

While studying the Bible, it is helpful to use study tools. Everyone has searched for an elusive verse. Or pondered the meaning of a verse obscured by the customs and languages of Bible times. Or perhaps wondered how to translate Bible measurements into present-day standards. There are several basic reference books that can help in the problems that arise in Bible study. Any serious, systematic study of the Bible will demand certain study helps and a guided plan of approach.

THE BIBLE ITSELF

The first requirement for Bible study is a study or reference Bible. The King James Version has been the most popular English Bible for hundreds of years. As discussed in the previous study, however, there are several trustworthy translations available. The Bible should be your most frequently used and favorite tool for study. It is, therefore, important to choose a Bible that is understandable to you and one with a print size that can be read without difficulty.

1. Read 2 Timothy 4:13. What example does Paul set for us regarding his appreciation of the Scriptures in this passage?

____

____

Another consideration when selecting a Bible is the paper quality. Some individuals like to make notes and highlight or underline key verses when studying. It is important to carefully select a Bible with paper that is not so thin that the markings distort the print on the other side of the page.

There are many study or reference Bibles which are widely used today. It would be impossible to highlight all of them in this study, but a brief description of several is included. Proper selection of a study Bible should include an evaluation of the helps provided in each version. Choose the one which is best suited to your study habits.

The *Thompson Chain Reference Bible* is a thorough and helpful work with a host of notes in the margin and an excellent Condensed Cyclopedia covering thousands of topics and text. It also contains information on the canon of Scripture and the principal English versions, an outlined analysis of each book of the Bible, a number of maps, a concordance, and an index. It also has a good harmony of the four Gospels and several excellent charts as well as an archaeological supplement.

The *Full Life Study Bible* identifies and recognizes the influence and power of the Holy Spirit in Scripture. It includes a center column cross-reference system, extensive study notes written from a Pentecostal/Charismatic perspective, charts, maps, subject index, and a concordance. It has a theme system which highlights 12 specific themes and directs the reader to the next text on that particular theme. It also provides 77 articles dealing with critical subjects in a more comprehensive manner than the notes.

Several other Bibles should be mentioned for your evaluation such as the *Life Application Bible, The New Open Bible,* and *The Emphasized Bible* by Rotherham.

It would be good to note that with the popularity of more recent translations (NIV, NASB, NKJV, and CEV) most of the above mentioned study Bibles are available in your favorite Bible translation. Some, like *The NIV Study Bible*, have been developed specifically for one version. Remember, evaluate and compare the study Bibles available. Determine what combination of helps will be of greatest benefit to your studies. If your decision is made carefully and prayerfully, you will be pleasantly surprised. The proper selection of a Bible will make your study very delightful and productive.

With the prevalence of computer usage, computer Bibles have become more popular. Software packages usually include one or more Bible translations with some predetermined study helps. They range from simple DOS-based packages to sophisticated systems running in Windows, Mac, or on CD-ROMs. An excellent choice is the *Logos Bible Software* which takes full advantage of the Windows environment. Other notables are the *Thompson Chain HyperBible, Biblesoft PC Study Bible, Biblesoft PC Reference Library, QuickVerse 2.0 DOS* by Parsons Technology, and the *macBible 3.0*. Each of these comes with an assortment of translations and study tools. A word of caution when purchasing Bible software—carefully research the packages which are available. As with a printed Bible, consider your current and future desires for Bible study and purchase the package which is best suited to your needs and which will run on your system.

2. Which Bible translation do you currently use?

3. What features mentioned in this study does it have?

4. Are there other features you would like to have in your Bible?

BIBLE STUDY TOOLS

Bible study tools vary in type and scholarly depth. It would be impossible to cover the ever-growing field of Bible reference material. Instead, an explanation of seven general types of study tools will provide an overview of what is available to those who desire a deeper understanding of God's Word. All tools listed in this study are well within the grasp of the average student of the Bible.

Margin References

Although references in a Bible appear in various ways, the most common is the center reference column. Other methods are the side column reference, references under each verse, or at the bottom of the page. Where they are located is simply a matter of personal preference. The most important thing is to familiarize yourself with them and use them as often as possible. Then they will contribute to meaningful and productive Bible study.

Subject references lead the reader from one mention of a truth to another. Some Bibles list the first and last references each time. This enables the reader to follow the subject from beginning to end at whatever point it is encountered in the Bible. Other systems simply direct the reader to another passage with a similar theme or different view on a theme without indicating the first or last. Regardless of the system, the objective is to provide the reader with additional text in the Bible to clarify a particular subject.

5. Read Romans 1:16. Record below the path your Bible directs you on for clarification of the word "gospel" or the phrase in which it is found.

Another help found in marginal references is alternative renderings of a word, phrase, or verse. The margin may also contain explanations of money, time, weights, etc. General statistical, geographical, and language information also is given in some Bibles.

Concordance

One of the foremost tools for Bible study is a concordance. A concordance provides immediate access to any verse of Scripture if one remembers only a part of it, even just a word. Simply stated, a concordance is an alphabetical listing of key words used in the Bible along with all Scripture references where they are found. Three concordances are recognized leaders in the field—*Cruden's Unabridged Concordance*, *Young's Analytical Concordance of the Bible*, and *Strong's Exhaustive Concordance of the Bible*. The last two are complete. For those who cannot afford a concordance it would be well to choose a Bible that contains one. Some Bibles have excellent concordances.

Students of the Bible will also find useful reference books which arrange subjects in topical fashion. *Nave's Topical Bible* is a sort of concordance with texts in full, a digest of 20,000 topics and subtopics, with more than 100,000 associated Scripture references. This resource enables you to find all the Scripture references related to one particular topic.

6. Look up the word "miracle" in your Bible's concordance or a separate concordance. List some of the references given.

____

____

____

Bible Dictionary And Encyclopedia

Another very important aid to Bible study is a dictionary of the Bible. Like any dictionary, it is an alphabetically arranged compilation of words and their definition, but they are words with biblical significance. Included with proper nouns—the names of persons and places—are common nouns with scriptural meanings. A helpful feature of some Bible dictionaries and encyclopedias is their use of pictures.

Through use of the dictionary and encyclopedia the student gets a clearer understanding of difficult words and unfamiliar names of persons, places, and things. An example of discoveries made through a Bible dictionary include the cubit: a measurement of nearly 18 inches. The penny is discovered to be the translation of the Greek word *denarius* which was the chief Roman silver coin and was worth about 15 to 17 cents or the equivalent of a day's wages. The common noun *stone* is treated with its particular biblical significance, with reference made to the places where the word appears. It will be found that the "hind" is a deer. The word *publican* is defined as the collector of Roman revenue who was hated among the Jews for his fraudulent exactions under the vicious Roman system.

Some of the better known dictionaries are *Unger's Bible Dictionary, The New Bible Dictionary* by Douglas, *The Eerdmans' Bible Dictionary*, and *The New International Dictionary of the Bible* by Douglas and Tenney. Two excellent, yet also more expensive, encyclopedias are the *International Standard Bible Encyclopedia* in five volumes and *The Zondervan Pictorial Encyclopedia of the Bible* by Tenney.

Bible Atlas

Though of secondary importance, a good Bible atlas greatly assists in Bible study. Most contain maps, charts, or pictures of the ruins of ancient civilizations, interesting views of landforms important to biblical happenings, and general information on biblical geography, geology, and archaeology.

A Bible atlas helps in visualizing the setting of great events of Scripture. The missionary journeys of Paul, the ministry of Jesus (and later, of His disciples), as well as the journeys of Abraham take on enriched meaning to the student who has a knowledge of the geography of the lands involved.

A good atlas is *Baker's Bible Atlas*. Another used by many is *The MacMillan Bible Atlas*.

Manners And Customs

Interesting and exciting books on biblical manners and customs are available and will make a substantial contribution to Bible study. Most Christians are unfamiliar with the cultural patterns of people who live in Eastern countries. When the

Holy Spirit moved on those who wrote the Scriptures, they expressed divine truth in language common to the people of their time and region. They used common objects and customs of their day to illustrate the message.

The purpose of books on biblical culture is to help us visualize and understand some of these objects and customs. When this occurs our understanding of biblical truth is greatly enhanced and enriched. An example of this can be drawn from Deuteronomy 22:8. Review of a Bible handbook reveals that the Palestinian homes were built with flat roofs. Since the people of that day spent considerable time on their roofs, it was necessary to build a parapet or railing to guard against accidents. Knowledge of this custom will greatly assist the student in understanding this verse.

Manners and Customs in the Bible by Matthews is a well-respected volume on this subject. Another excellent book is *The Land and the Book* by Thomson. Both of these enhance Bible study by illuminating the trends of Bible times.

A Bible handbook is a valuable tool for study as well. It may duplicate information in other types of books and could be an alternative for those who do not wish to invest in a number of books. *Halley's Bible Handbook*, as an example, is a mine of general Bible information.

7. How does your cultural background affect your understanding of the Bible?

---

8. How would your interpretation of Scripture differ from someone's from another part of the world or even a different part of your own country?

---

9. Have you ever experienced an intercultural friendship? How did you build that relationship despite your differences?

Commentary

A Bible commentary, as implied by its name, comments on the Bible, passage by passage, and verse by verse, interpreting its meaning. For hundreds of years,

Bible scholars and spiritual leaders have recorded the results of their studies and much of this has been gathered in various commentaries. Some commentaries are the work of a single author, while others are a compilation of the efforts of a number of individuals. Commentaries may range in size from one volume to well over 50 volumes.

Since a commentary is written for the purpose of interpreting Scripture, care should be taken in selecting one. Three of the better-known concise commentaries are *Matthew Henry's Commentary on the Whole Bible*, *The Wycliffe Bible Commentary*, and the *Evangelical Commentary on the Bible*. A good commentary set is *The Complete Biblical Library* which is accompanied by a Greek-English dictionary set and a harmony of the Gospels. The *New International Commentary on the New Testament and the Old Testament* and the *Tyndale Old and New Testament Commentary* are good sets which can be purchased one volume at a time. It is always good to remember that sets of commentaries, like the last two mentioned, will include works which are very strong and others that may be lacking in their depth of study. With these works it is advisable to be particular in your selections.

Bible Software Study Tools

As mentioned earlier in this study, we are in an age of high computer usage. Many of the study tools highlighted are available in computer software. Some of the tools, like a concordance or dictionary, may be provided with a basic package while others can be added. Helps that are available (depending on the system purchased) are: *Nave's Topical Bible*, a Greek/Hebrew dictionary, *The Treasury of Scripture Knowledge*, a Bible atlas, maps, and *Matthew Henry's Commentary on the Whole Bible* to name just a few. Once again examine the possibilities and choose software which will best meet your needs.

SUMMARY

There is a great variety of tools available to the serious Bible student. As mentioned, study Bibles are available in many translations and versions. Concordances and dictionaries have been produced to complement those choices. Computer software can be found for Scripture text as well as a magnitude of study tools. Dictionaries and encyclopedias help clarify difficult words and unfamiliar people, places, and things. Atlases and books on the practices of Bible times provide insight into the culture of the biblical authors. Commentaries provide, explain, or interpret information of the Bible.

The list provided in this study is not intended to be all-inclusive and may not necessarily give the best title in a given field. Parallel Bibles offer the convenience of two or more versions in one volume. Language helps provide better understanding of the original texts. Word studies facilitate in-depth research. This is only an attempt to provide basic assistance to those who are interested in developing a Bible study library.

Remember, Bibles with explanatory notes and research tools are convenient and prove helpful, but notes and tools should not take the place of the Word itself. Bible reading, independent of notes and commentary, cannot be overemphasized. Study tools are good but should not detract from our focus, which should be on Scripture itself.

LET'S REVIEW

1. List three study Bibles suggested in this study. What are the advantages of each?

2. How can a Bible dictionary enrich your Bible study?

3. How does one use a concordance? a Bible atlas? a commentary?

4. Why is it beneficial to be familiar with the customs and practices of the people of Bible times?

5. What is the most important tool for Bible study?

Study 4

Preparing Yourself For Study

Spiritual success for both an individual and a church can come only through Bible study and reflection. A greater use and deeper understanding of the Word of God by believers is essential to a living, dynamic church. D. L. Moody said, "I never saw a useful Christian who was not a student of the Bible. If a man neglects his Bible, he may pray and ask God to use him in his work, but God cannot make much use of him; for there is not much for the Holy Spirit to work upon. We must have the Word itself, which is sharper than any two-edged sword."

The Bible should be studied systematically. A knowledge of the Bible, or any one book of the Bible, comes by a definite plan of reading and studying. This study examines the personal preparation needed to implement such a plan and maximize its spiritual benefits.

PRELIMINARY STEPS

Read Proverbs 2:1-5

Personal Bible study is a battle. One does not find too many people today who seek a quiet place with a book; their number is even fewer when it comes to Bible study. There are countless distractions, and time runs short.

Christians need to evaluate how they spend their time. Unwise use of time is one of the greatest deterrents to Christian growth.

Bible study is the most effective tool of the Holy Spirit to bring the Christian into conformity to Christ. Understandably, Satan uses every device possible to keep Christians from the Word of God.

It is important to remember the words of F. B. Meyer, "There is no book that will so repay time spent on its pages as will the Word of God."

Let's turn our attention to seven rules drawn from Proverbs 2 which will assist us in our quest to study God's Word.

View The Bible As God's Word (Proverbs 2:1)

We must come to the Bible with the conviction that it is the Word of God through which God will surely speak to us. We do not need to prove the Bible first and then accept it; we accept it and then let it prove itself.

1. What does James 1:6,7 say about the effects of not accepting the authority of the Word of God?

____

____

2. What benefit of trusting the authority of God's Word is stated in 1 Thessalonians 2:13?

____

____

3. Is it possible to read the Bible and receive no benefit? Why or why not? (Hebrews 4:2).

____

____

____

Obedience Is Required (Proverbs 2:1)

The soul must be exercised by the Word. The Word must school us and change our lives. If we fail to translate the Word into daily practice, we will be spiritually anemic. Bible study brings renewed devotion to God. Even more, it produces discipline and determination resulting in the transformation of human nature. There is no better way to blind ourselves to Bible truth than to refuse to heed and obey it.

✎ **4. According to Hosea 4:6, what is the destiny of those who fail to obtain godly knowledge?**

____

✎ **5. According to James 1:22-25, mental knowledge is not sufficient for the Christian. Cite at least one example of how you have put God's Word into action.**

____

____

Listening Is Demanded (Proverbs 2:2)

The word used here means to "listen," to "take heed." We need to incline or turn our ears to the voice of the Holy Spirit. A first principle in Bible study is to learn to read intelligently. But more than that, we need the illumination of the Holy Spirit, for the Bible is a revelation of spiritual truth, and its understanding is dependent upon spiritual sensitivity. Consider every phrase, every word of Scripture. Let the Holy Spirit make it real to the listening ear.

✎ **6. What promise is made concerning illumination in John 16:13?**

____

____

The Heart Must Be Yielded (Proverbs 2:2)

Heart-searching should precede Bible study. In Scripture, the Word has been likened to seed. We must prepare the soil of our hearts to receive the seed of the Word so it will bear fruit.

✎ **7. Our attitude must be correct if we are to receive from God's Word. Read the following passages and record the required attitude described in each.**

Psalm 139:23,24 ____________________________________

John 3:3 ____

Matthew 11:25 _____________________________________

Psalm 119:97 ______________________________________

Psalm 119:100 _____________________________________

We need to open our hearts to God and let Him prepare them to receive the truth of His Word.

Prayer Is Necessary (Proverbs 2:3)

We cannot, by our wisdom, understand the Bible. In all our study we must carefully seek the help of the Holy Spirit. He alone can remove the veil from our minds. It is impossible to know the Bible without prayer. We need to echo the Psalmist's prayer recorded in Psalm 119:18.

8. Write out the Psalmist's prayer (Psalm 119:18) and commit it to memory.

When we breathe this prayer in faith, we can expect the Lord to open our understanding as He did for the disciples after His resurrection (Luke 24:45) and for Lydia, the seller of purple (Acts 16:14).

Seek As For Silver (Proverbs 2:4)

Silver is a standard of money. People will do most anything for money because money gives them so many of the things they want. People work for the paycheck. But there is something of far greater worth than the silver of this world.

**9. How does King David view the words of Scripture? (Psalm 12:6).**

As a person disciplines himself to hard work to get a share of this world's goods, the Christian must prepare for the discipline of businesslike Bible study, coupled with businesslike prayer. It takes earnestness of purpose, concentration of effort, and determination of mind and heart.

It is a good practice to begin each day with the study and understanding of a biblical passage, then to find ways of applying it to your life that day. This transforms God's Word from words on a page to reality and life.

Search As For Hidden Treasure (Proverbs 2:4)

The word "search" is equivalent to dig. One translation (Vulgate) reads "to dig out." The treasures of God's Word are to be found by the one who will diligently dig for them. We need to use the same untiring energy with which we would dig for hidden treasure in our search for the riches of the Word. The perseverance of the seeker after material wealth often puts to shame the seeker after spiritual wealth. This matter of searching is important.

10. What should result from diligent Bible study?

Proverbs 2:5 ______________________________

____

1 Corinthians 2:14 ______________________________

____

PRACTICAL STEPS

Read Psalm 119:97-104

God wants us to study the Bible. He has provided the Book and the Teacher (the Holy Spirit). Through His servants, we have an abundance of help in the form of Bible study books and study methods. If we have a desire to know the Word, a willingness to give time for that purpose, and a resolve to keep on despite obstacles, we will find the joy of learning and living in the Word. Come hungry to the Word, for the spiritually hungry are never disappointed by God.

11. Write out Christ's promise to you which is found in Matthew 5:6.

____

____

Read Psalm 119:97. Notice the personal pronoun, I. Bible study will be tedious until it becomes personal. Then it can be delightful, intensely interesting, thrilling, profitable. In Bible study we must be participators rather than spectators.

Bible study requires a systematic approach. Do not stay only with those portions which have brought blessing or seem more inviting. If a less interesting passage falls into the plan, resist the inclination to skip over it.

12. Read 2 Timothy 3:16 and Matthew 4:4. What do these verses suggest about the importance of a systematic study of the Bible?

____

____

Aim to cover all the Bible. Approach the uninviting passage with a real spirit of study. Pray over it—meditate upon it—compare it with parallel passages—read what others have written about it. Watch it become real!

Actual study should involve reading the passage or the book over again and again. Read available translations. Make notes for later study. Keep a record of your observations just as they occur to you, whether they seem significant or not.

13. **How would the following practices help foster a better understanding of Scripture?**

Reading the passage or book over and over.

____

____

____

Utilizing various Bible translations.

____

____

____

Keeping a journal or making notes of your insights.

____

____

____

Writing down your thoughts will help to stimulate thinking and concentration. You discover how little you know when you try to write it down. Use a study Bible that can be marked. Marking your Bible will help to make your reading more concrete. Try underlining passages which are especially meaningful. Jot in the margins thoughts which the Spirit makes real.

PROGRESSIVE STEPS

Read 2 Timothy 3:16

Effective Bible study involves the following sequence of questions: (1) Observation—what does the passage say (content)? (2) Interpretation—what does it mean? (3) Application—how does it apply to me? What does it say to me (personal application)? What does it say to me today (relevant personal application)? What am I going to do about it today (immediate personal action on the Word)? It is necessary to observe carefully what the passage actually says before interpreting it, and then to apply the truths personally.

A simple, practical approach to study is suggested in 2 Timothy 3:16. Just as John 3:16 gives us the central verse of the Bible on how to become a Christian, 2 Timothy 3:16 gives us an important verse on how to grow as a Christian.

Any passage in the Bible—a verse, a chapter, a book—is God's Word and is profitable in four ways.

14. List the four ways in 2 Timothy 3:16 that God's Word is profitable.

Bible study should not only be systematic in its mechanics but it should also be systematic in its practice. Bible study should be a regular feature of our daily schedule.

15. Bible study has been compared to eating. How might the two be similar? Compare physical food/nourishment to spiritual food/nourishment.

If we expect to stay alive, we must keep feeding ourselves. We do not eat a week's supply of food for the natural body in a day; there must be a daily consumption of food. Neither can we absorb enough Bible study in a day to last for a lengthy period of time. If spiritual strength is to be maintained, there must be constant feeding on the Word of God.

What we learn in Bible study must be passed on to others (2 Timothy 2:2). Unless we do this our study can become dull and uninteresting. It is the constant outflow of water from a body of water that keeps it fresh and free from the stagnant odors and scum of a dead body of water.

We use what we have learned by sharing it with others. Let's take the good things the Lord has shown us and bring a blessing to someone else. Sharing is an excellent way to make a truth real to us.

16. Read 2 Timothy 2:2. Some think that teaching only occurs in the classroom. This is not the case. List practical ways you can share information gained through your study of the Bible with others.

Let's Review

1. How can one prepare for Bible study? Why is preparation important?

2. What part does the Holy Spirit play in Bible study? Explain.

3. Compare the importance of John 3:16 and 2 Timothy 3:16.

4. Name some principles to follow in Bible study.

5. Why should we present what we learn to others?

STUDY 5

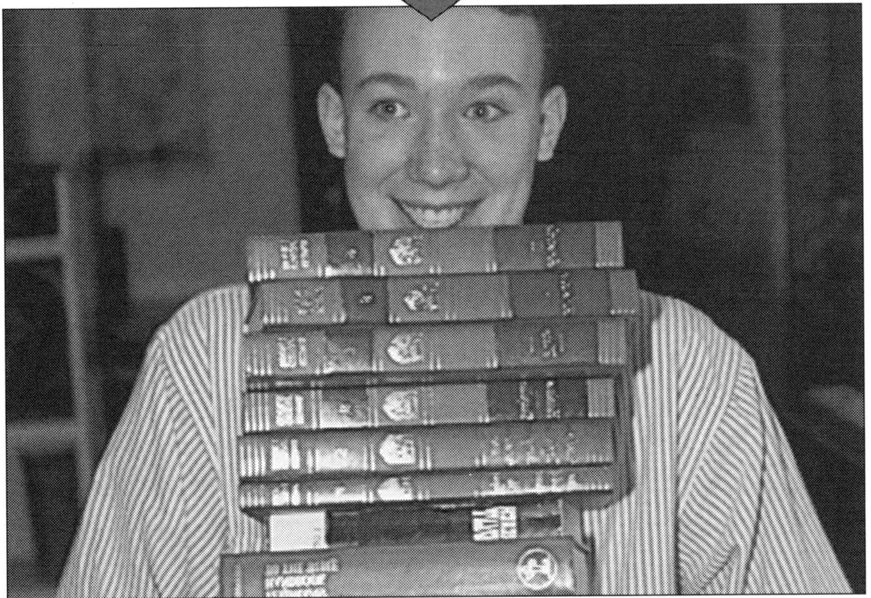

IDENTIFYING VARIOUS TYPES OF BIBLICAL LITERATURE

As modern readers, we understand there are various types of literature available. A cookbook assists in the construction of a good meal. In a novel, the author utilizes a variety of story lines to proclaim his/her view of some universal principle. Text-books are designed to authoritatively teach a body of factual information. Poetry allows the reader's emotions to soar to great heights and plunge to great depths.

It is important for Christians to be able to recognize the various genres of literature in the Bible and to interpret these genres correctly. Failing to recognize literary differences in the Bible will lead to misinterpretation and can lead to false doctrine or shattered hope. In this study, we will explore the major types of literature present in the Bible and provide insights into their proper interpretation.

THE OLD TESTAMENT NARRATIVE

The most common type of literature found in the Bible is the narrative. Over 40% of the Old Testament is this type of literature. The term *narrative* is used rather than *story* to avoid confusion with the common equation of story with fiction. The biblical narrative is an entirely true story of an historical event.

Common elements of all narratives are plot and characters. It is important to read an entire story to discover the point the author is trying to portray. Individual details of a narrative are not as important as an understanding of the overriding theme of the story.

No individual biblical narrative stands alone. Gordon D. Fee and Douglas Stuart, in *How To Read The Bible For All Its Worth*, state there are three levels of Old Testament narrative: the top, the middle, and the bottom. The top level is referred to as "redemptive history" providing information which explains God's universal plan. The middle level consists of narratives that illuminate Israel as a nation. The lower level is made up of stories depicting individual struggles and successes. The lower level stories are woven together to create the middle and top level narratives.

The narratives of the Bible are specifically chosen by God to tell His story. Each story illustrates a specific principle, but we should not end our understanding there. Lower level narratives should always be seen in the context of the larger story.

Each narrative provides a different insight into God's universal truth. Like a diamond, redemptive history is multifaceted. One story could never reveal all the truth. Each of the biblical narratives cast light at a unique angle thus displaying more of God's divine plan.

1. Read Genesis 17. How does this story work on the 3 levels just described?

What does the story tell the reader about Abraham and his temporal family?

____

____

____

What does the story teach about the nation of Israel?

____

____

____

What does the reader learn about the universal redemptive plan of God?

____

____

____

A mistake made by many, when interpreting narratives, is to attempt to supply facts which the author chose not to include. Narratives are not meant to be exhaustive. They simply illustrate a point which God has clearly taught elsewhere. Putting words into the author's mouth is dangerous. God gave us all we need to understand each story. Allow the story to speak for itself.

Things to remember when interpreting a narrative:

•A narrative usually illustrates a previously revealed truth rather than proclaiming a new truth.

•A narrative tells a story as it happened. There is no reason to think we should model our lives after the main characters in the narrative. The action of a character neither demands nor gives us permission to copy the action. The overall point (focus) of the narrative is more important than the individual characters.

•A narrative seldom, if ever, gives all the details of the story in question. The details given are the details the author wished the reader to know. Do not violate the author's will by guessing what was meant or fill in the gaps with modern speculation.

•A narrative is not an allegory. Read the story for its clear meaning rather than spiritualizing its meaning.

Each narrative provides a piece in the giant puzzle which comprises God's universal plan of redemption. The more pieces we discover, the more fully we will understand our Heavenly Father.

BIBLICAL POETRY

Poetry is found throughout the Bible. The highest concentration of biblical poetry is found in the Psalms. Whereas most of the literature of the Bible communicates truth from God to man, the poetry found in the Psalms are prayers and hymns addressed to God, or are expressions of man concerning God through song. Biblical poetry should not be viewed as expressions of doctrinal truth, but as instruments to aid us in our worship of God. Biblical poetry compels the reader to express praise or contemplate God's greatness.

Poetry, as found in the Psalms, has a variety of purposes. The lament is designed to help individuals express their suffering and heartbreak. A common lament is the imprecatory psalm—requesting God to destroy an enemy.

2. Read Psalm 83.

What does the Psalmist request in this psalm?

____

____

What emotions are evident?

____

____

Many have reacted negatively to imprecatory psalms, citing God's command that we forgive. The imprecatory psalm teaches us that we are free to express all emotions to God, providing we leave the anger there. Other types of poetry found in the Psalms are songs of trust, celebration, thanksgiving, and royal psalms. Understanding the type of psalm will aid in proper interpretation.

3. Find the reference listed in the first column. After reading the psalm, identify its type by matching it to the list in the second column.

____**Psalm 50**	**a. A Lament**
____**Psalm 138**	**b. A Song Of Trust**
____**Psalm 27**	**c. Celebration**
____**Psalm 3**	**d. Thanksgiving**
____**Psalm 18**	**e. A Royal Psalm**

Things to remember when interpreting biblical poetry:

•Parallelism is a common feature in biblical poetry.

a. Synonymous Parallelism—The same thought is expressed in a different way in two consecutive lines of poetry. An example can be found in Psalm 19.

b. Antithetical Parallelism—A thought is expressed in the first line of poetry, and the second line contrasts the thought of the first. An example can be found in Hosea 7:14.

c. Synthetic Parallelism—A thought is expressed in the first line, and an extension or expansion of the thought is expressed in the second. An example can be found in Psalm 27.

•Biblical poetry speaks to the emotions rather than to the mind. Poetry is designed to elicit an emotional response rather than provide a doctrinal statement.

•Poetry is purposely metaphorical. The reader should look for the spiritual meaning.

•Poetry must be seen as a literary unit. Do not attempt to understand an isolated verse. To properly understand a psalm, one must understand the entire psalm.

Biblical poetry is refreshment for the soul. It is vital that as we study the Bible we do not demand more from the poetry than was intended by God.

WISDOM LITERATURE

Wisdom literature is primarily found in the books of Job, Proverbs, Song of Solomon, and Ecclesiastes. Wisdom literature is unique in that it provides a perspective on life as it is meant to be. The term *wisdom* refers to the individual who lives close to God rather than an individual of superior intelligence. Wisdom literature is one of the most misunderstood genres in the Bible. Individuals are often guilty of creating concrete doctrines from material intended as general principles for living.

Things to remember when interpreting wisdom literature:

•Individual proverbs should not be viewed as guarantees from God. Proverbs are general principles which when applied will generally lead to a predictable result. Basing one's life and hopes on a specific proverb is dangerous, and may lead to disappointment and confusion.

•A piece of wisdom literature should be read as a collection. Individual sections from the Book of Job, Ecclesiastes, or the Song of Solomon taken out of context can lead individuals to beliefs which are out of step with the rest of Scripture.

4. Read Job 14:7-12.

If a person read this passage in isolation, what would his/her conclusion be concerning eternal life?

How does this conflict with the greater biblical teaching?

How can the conflict be explained?

•Proverbs are meant to be remembered. Words were chosen to catch and maintain the attention of the reader. Proverbs employ hyperbolic, parabolic, and symbolic language. A demand for a literal interpretation of all proverbs and writings within the category of wisdom literature will lead to a misunderstanding of the writer's original intent. It is imperative to understand the intent of the writer.

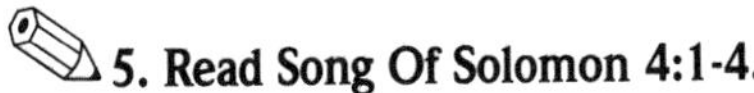

5. Read Song Of Solomon 4:1-4.

Sketch a portrait of the desirable woman based on the literal description.

How does this illustrate the danger of interpreting figurative language literally?

____

____

____

Prophetic Literature

Prophetic utterances have for centuries captured the interest of mankind, particularly Christians. Faulty interpretation, even by some evangelical scholars, has caused much misunderstanding.

Generally, Bible students recognize two aspects of prophecy, "foretelling" and "forthtelling." Foretelling is the prediction of future events. Forthtelling means exhortation, instruction, or reproof.

It is imperative to properly interpret prophetic passages. Many people find this difficult because they do not follow general rules for determining the meaning of prophecies. A multitude of complex laws or rules could be overwhelming, but a few essential suggestions could prove helpful.

Things to remember when interpreting prophecy:

- Make a careful analysis of the passage within its context. Determine the meanings of all words, and learn as much as possible about the background of the prophet and the people to whom the prophecy was directed. Analyze the passage in light of the events that preceded it and those that followed.
- It is of special significance to identify clearly the people for whom the prophecy is intended.
- Make certain you thoroughly understand the prophetic message.
- If it has been fulfilled, be able to correlate the prophecy with the fulfillment. Identify clearly the prophetic elements in the prophet's message with the corresponding ones in the fulfillment.
- When you don't understand do not try to force a solution. Remember, we don't know everything. And some prophetic messages still have an element of mystery to them. There are answers, but we haven't discovered them all yet.

Typology

Typology makes an interesting study. It is based on historical connections. In typology the interpreter finds a correspondence between a person, event, thing, or institution in the Old Testament and one in the New Testament. For our purposes, we will compare aspects of the Old Testament with the New Testament, although there are instances of types and antitypes within one Testament only.

A type is a person, event, thing, or institution in biblical history for which there is a later fulfillment. The Holy Spirit, as the Author of Scripture, placed within the type a prefiguration of what would later be identified as the antitype or the fulfillment. The antitype, then, is the person, event, thing, or institution appearing later that fulfills or corresponds to the type. We often say that Moses is a type of Christ.

Thus Moses is the type and Christ is the antitype. Only as the antitype is revealed is the fuller and deeper meaning of the type discerned.

Volumes have been written about typology. Some Bible students have made extreme and unwarranted use of types. But this does not detract from the beauty and reality revealed in them.

6. Read the passage associated with the antitype and match it to the Old Testament character or event.

Type	Antitype
____Moses	a. Christ (John 3:14)
____Brazen Serpent	b. Baptism (1 Peter 3:20,21)
____Melchizedek	c. Christ (Acts 3:19-26)
____Adam	d. Christ (Romans 5:12-21)
____Flood	e. Christ (Hebrews 5:5-9)
____Feasts of Israel	f. Aspects of Redemption (1 Corinthians 5:7)

Things to remember when interpreting types:

•The type must resemble the antitype and must be designed to resemble it. Be careful to not destroy the historical sense to establish the spiritual.

•Don't make details typical. As there is similitude between the type and the antitype there is also dissimilitude. No type is to be totally representative of the antitype.

THE PARABLE

Parables are an effective way to teach religious truth. They have been used for centuries by people the world over. Jesus made liberal use of parables during His earthly ministry. Usually His stories centered on situations common to His listeners. The themes focused on topics such as agriculture, marriage, family life, daily work, and the business world.

A parable is a story that employs an ordinary circumstance of life to illustrate a spiritual truth. Jesus used them to bring out the deeper mysteries of the kingdom of God. Those who were interested in His teachings searched out the meanings, and in the process gleaned deeper truth hidden to the natural mind. Curiosity seekers and His enemies found it extremely difficult to understand the spiritual truth taught by the parable.

Things to remember when interpreting parables:

•Seek to understand the earthly details of the story as it was related by the speaker or writer. Try to imagine the unfolding of the account as told to the original hearers.

•Try to ascertain as clearly as possible the attitude and spiritual condition of the original group to whom it was related.

•Seek to understand the reason that prompted the speaker to use the parable. It should be remembered that Jesus did not always employ parables to teach others. He used a variety of methods.

•Look for the literal details of the story. When this has been accomplished, pinpoint the central message.

•Relate the central message to the spiritual emphasis of the speaker or writer.

SIMILES

A simile is a figure of speech in which two essentially unlike things are compared. The comparison is usually made by using the words *as* or *like*. Jesus made liberal use of similes in vivid descriptions. They require little research, but prayerful concentration. It is critical in approaching a simile to clearly understand the two things being compared.

7. Read John 10:1-18.

Identify the contrasting elements in this passage.

____

____

____

Summarize the principle being taught through this simile.

____

____

____

THE EPISTLE

An epistle is another name for a letter. The New Testament contains a great deal of this literary genre. Some make a distinction between personal letters and universal epistles. A quick review of the apostle Paul's letters will reveal the distinction. This technical difference does not change the importance of the writing or the manner in which the letter is interpreted.

An epistle provides a great deal of theology but never represents all of the author's theology. New Testament epistles were written on specific occasions to deal with specific issues. When studying the epistles, we must identify the occasion that necessitated the letter and then determine the principles outlined by the author.

Letters today can be identified at a glance. When we see a date, return address, salutation, body, and signature, we know we are looking at a letter. The first century epistle could be identified by looking for six elements; the name of the writer, the name of the recipient, a greeting, a prayer wish or thanksgiving, a body, and a farewell.

8. Read 1 Peter. Identify with references the six elements of the epistle.

author ____________________

recipient ____________________

greeting ____________________

prayer/thanksgiving ____________________

body ____________________

farewell ____________________

Proper understanding of the epistle requires the employment of "exegesis." *Exegesis* means "born out of" or "to come out of." Exegesis demands that we allow the text to speak to us rather than reading thoughts and ideas into the text.

Things to remember when interpreting an epistle:

•Reconstruct the history of the time by reading about the city in a Bible dictionary or in the background section of a commentary dealing with the selected epistle.

•Read the entire letter in one setting. Seldom does a person, today, receive a letter and read only certain sections. We read the whole letter to fully understand the message of the writer. Epistles can only be fully understood when they are read in their entirety.

•While reading through the letter, determine the occasion or problem which compelled the author to write the letter.

•Create an outline mapping the major thoughts of the author.

•Read each paragraph of each major outline point. Ask, "Why did the author include this paragraph, and how does it help develop the author's overall argument?"

•Summarize the author's argument into a 1- or 2-sentence principle statement.

•Ask, how may I apply this principle to my personal life?

There will be some portions of an epistle that seem too difficult to understand using these suggestions. After exhausting your own resources, it is acceptable to consult a good commentary.

SUMMARY

The scope of this study does not allow an in-depth treatment of each literary form found in Scripture. The genres most often employed have been highlighted. The Bible is a library of literary works, inspired by God. It is helpful to be able to identify the type of literature God chose to communicate His truth, and then utilize the appropriate methods of interpretation.

LET'S REVIEW

1. Why is it important to recognize the various types of biblical literature?

2. Identify and explain the 3 levels of biblical narrative.

3. Identify and explain the 3 types of parallelism employed in biblical poetry.

4. What is a proverb and what is its function?

5. What six components form the structure of a first century epistle?

Study 6

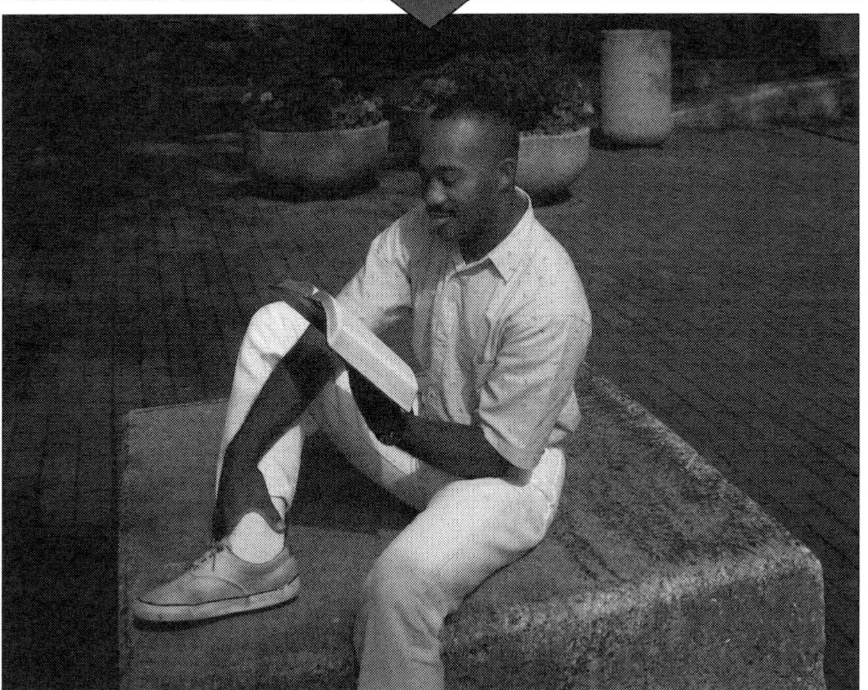

Surveying The Books Of The Bible

Many books of the Bible remain ineffectual in the lives of their readers because they have never caught the broad scope of truth contained in those books. Readers need the sense of the whole of Scripture before they seek to understand the parts.

One of the best approaches to understanding the Bible as a whole is Bible synthesis. Synthetic study simply means the study of the Bible as a whole, each book of the Bible as a whole, and each book as seen in its relation to the other books. Synthesis is the opposite of analysis. By analysis we take an object apart to examine its parts; by synthesis we put it together and consider it as a whole.

OBTAINING BACKGROUND MATERIAL

Many people believe the Bible is a book one can open anywhere and it will reveal its storehouse of truth. Such a practice will reveal some truth to the casual reader, but it will not give him the full message. To understand the Bible properly, one must grasp a comprehensive picture of its fundamental purpose.

There are certain things to look for when reading a book of the Bible. It is important to determine the author, scope, occasion, theme, time, place, and the form of the text. Each of these will assist in understanding the full message being presented.

Before reading through the selected book for the first time, it will help to search out significant background information. This will contribute appreciably to one's understanding of the book.

To understand a book it is important to learn who the author is and what can be known about him. For instance, a study of Paul, Peter, and John will reveal interesting facts about them. They could be called apostles of the three cardinal graces. Paul might be called the apostle of faith, Peter the apostle of hope, and John the apostle of love. Their lives, their actions, and their writings emphasize these lines of truth.

Determining the date and place the book was written and to whom it was written will be helpful also. Once we have this information, it can be used to help us become familiar with the social, moral, and political conditions at the time of the writing. We can determine the circumstance which led to the writing of the book. Each piece of information improves our view of the purpose of this book in the overall message of the Bible.

Most of the widely accepted study Bibles contain this type of background information and more. Often it is condensed and summarized on one or two pages. Some even include a book outline. This makes it convenient for those who do not have the time or reference books necessary to search out the information.

1. Use a study Bible or reference materials to discover the author, basic background information, date, and place of writing of 1 Corinthians. Record your findings below.

____

____

____

____

READING FOR UNDERSTANDING

The Bible is the Word of God. Therefore it is necessary for us to learn what it is and what it means. We must know the contents of the Bible before we can know its interpretation. In other words, we must know what the Bible says before we can understand what it means. A first step will be to acquire knowledge of the factual content of the Scriptures. Next we will need to see the unity of the Bible, the relationship of one book to another, and each to the whole. Further, we will need to see Christ and His redemption in all the Bible. Finally, we must make a personal application of the truths which we have learned to our own lives.

Reading the Bible is necessary and profitable, but it is not enough. The Bible must be studied systematically. No doubt, most Christians read a daily portion of Scripture as a devotional exercise. This is good and right. But too many read the Bible in portions and never read it in any other way. The Bible requires study. Its hidden depths will not be revealed to the superficial reader. Jesus told His antagonists to "search the Scriptures." The word "search" is a strong word indicating the use of energy, diligence, and application to the task. The prospector searches for treasure; the hunter searches for prey; the police search for the lawbreaker; the posse searches for the lost child. In like manner, we must employ a law of diligence and thoroughness in our searching of the Scriptures.

When we read the Bible for purposes of study it is not enough to read one book and pass on to another. The same book must be read repeatedly—possibly a half dozen times until the message grips us and begins to reveal its secrets to us. Many people read the Bible, even study it, but they do not get a grip on it. They fail to gain a working knowledge of its contents. To avoid this frustration we could adopt a plan of reading, rereading, and reading again a Bible book until its message becomes a part of us. We will get a grip on the book, or rather the book will get a grip on us.

Many Christians struggle to develop a plan of maintaining interest in reading a book through at one sitting. They may find it difficult to grasp the teachings of the book in one reading, to note its construction, development, and purpose. It is important not to lose interest before beginning. Individuals need to find a way to read a text in the light of the context, and the context in the light of its relationship to the book, and the book in relation to the Bible as a whole.

Selection of the book to be studied is important. Almost every book was written because of some special need or circumstance and thus has a particular background and serves a given purpose. For example, the Pentateuch (first five books of the Old Testament) lays a foundation of historical fact for the books that follow. In similar fashion, the Book of Romans lays a foundation for the Church and its doctrines. A grasp of Romans with its development of the great doctrine of justification by faith—the foundation truth of all Christian doctrine—makes it possible for the believer to have a life of daily victory.

It will probably be best to begin your study with First Thessalonians, First Peter, or First John. After the book has been chosen, begin by prayerfully reading it through. All the New Testament Epistles, except Romans, First and Second Corinthians, and Hebrews, can be read in half an hour or less. If you keep this in mind, you will not be as easily discouraged at the task. Your reading should not be hurried either. Many times your study will involve much time poring over a few verses, or even just a word or two. This is appropriate but your first course of action should be to read through the entire book in one sitting. Give Bible reading a fair chance and it will become fascinating as the Holy Spirit begins to illuminate the Word.

2. Read John 14:26. What is promised about the ministry of the Holy Spirit?

____

____

____

The first reading of a book may not leave much of an impression. But faithful, prayerful, and systematic reading will not be fruitless. Soon details will begin to take shape in your mind. Persistent reading of a book will give you a familiarity with it and help you handle it freely.

On a second or third reading certain things will become evident. It may be that often repeated expressions come to your attention. For instance, there is the key word *better* in Hebrews which is used to portray the contrast of the good things of Judaism and the better things of Christ.

3. Trace the word *precious* as used by Peter in his two epistles and list the references below.

____

____

____

____

____

What truth is being illustrated by this key word?

____

____

Study with a pen in hand, underlining key words and writing out observations. Use a notebook to jot down the things which begin to become evident. Gradually, as you continue to read, an understanding of what the book is about will begin to form in your mind.

In pursuing the synthetic method of Bible study, you try first to discover the scope of a particular book. You will want to see the ground it covers and get a bird's-eye view of the subject it deals with so you can discover the purpose for which it was written. Every book has a theme and a purpose. The discovery of a key word or phrase can be the clue to the understanding of the purpose of the book. For instance, the key phrase of Romans is "the righteousness of God." Paul wrote this epistle for the purpose of making it plain to all that righteousness comes by God and from Him alone. The Church must guard against the error of salvation by works. This is the purpose and theme of Romans.

PUTTING IT ALL TOGETHER

The Word of God is different from all other books. There are no contradictions. Each book is a unified whole in itself. The 66 books of the Bible blend their themes together into a beautiful harmony. But how can 66 books written by about 40 authors over a period of approximately 1,600 years have perfect unity? The answer is simple. The Bible has perfect unity because it has one Author, the Holy Spirit, and He has the divine attribute of omniscience (all knowledge). Thus it was no great problem for the Holy Spirit, who knows all things, to inspire such diverse writings and still preserve unity.

One positive feature of the synthetic approach to Bible study is that it helps us to see this unity. The more books of the Bible we apply this study method to, the more clearly we will see the unity of the entire Bible. Often a truth has different aspects, but when the Bible deals with these, its message is not contradictory. All facets of the truth, when clearly viewed, form a beautiful pattern.

Seeing the unity of the Bible leads to understanding the interrelationships within the Bible. To begin to understand the relationships, we must determine the central theme of the Bible as a whole. Although it is expressed in varying terms, the Bible's central theme focuses on the redemption of sinful man through the divinely appointed Savior. Now, as we take a survey of individual books, we can ask ourselves how each relates to the Bible's central theme and the other books of the Bible.

It is good to look for the relationships between events, people, political institutions, prophecies, places, and teachings as well. Usually we will need to consciously look for relationships, but it is not unusual for the Bible to mention some in the normal flow of events.

4. Read 1 Corinthians 15:22. Note the Old and New Testament people mentioned in this verse and their relationship to each other.

____

____

5. Read Genesis 22:3-14. What is the relationship of this event to the crucifixion of Christ?

____

____

HOW IT WORKS

Let's take a survey and follow the procedures presented in this study. Some material will be gathered from notes from a study Bible or other reference books. Remember, it is only after repeated readings of any book of the Bible that we will begin to see the aim of the author and see the orderly pattern of the contents.

Which book are we going to study?

Genesis

Who is the human author of the book?

Undisclosed in the text of the book, it is historically attributed to Moses. In Luke 24:44 Jesus refers to the "Law of Moses," which includes the first five books of the Bible.

Who were the original recipients of this book?

The nation of Israel.

What is the occasion leading to and the date and place of the writing of the book?

The occasion leading to its writing was the need for a record of the beginning of the heavens and the earth, of plant, animal, and human life, relationships, and institutions.

The time and place of the writing are estimated to be during the time Israel was wandering in the wilderness between 1446 and 1406 B.C.

After reading through the book several times, what are some key words or expressions used by the author? List them with references.

The key word of Genesis is "generations" or "account," which includes such concepts as the birth, genealogy, and history of the major figures in Genesis. The word occurs in the following instances: 2:4; 5:1; 6:9; 10:1; 11:10; 11:27; 25:12; 25:19; 36:1; 37:2.

What are the purpose and theme of the book?

The purpose of Genesis is to reveal God's will and purpose in creation and redemption from the time of creation to the time of the beginning of His chosen nation Israel.

Genesis records the history of creation, the Fall, the Flood, and the beginning of nations. It relates the biographies of Abraham, Isaac, Jacob, and Joseph.

What are the key facts in the book? Use these to develop a brief outline.

Certain facts become quite obvious as we read Genesis. Note the following as they bring a sweeping picture of the book.

The first great fact is creation. This is covered in the first two chapters. Genesis 1 outlines the events of the 6 days of creation—(1) light; (2) atmosphere; (3) dry land, sea, plant life; (4) sun, moon, and stars; (5) fish and birds; (6) animals and man. The second chapter describes in greater detail the creation of man. This return to describe a matter in more detail is a pattern which the Holy Spirit uses again and again in the Bible. It is generally referred to as "the law of recurrence."

The second outstanding fact of Genesis is the Fall, the beginning of sin among men. Chapters 3 and 4 deal with this matter. Again one finds details which form an outline—the temptation by the serpent (3:1-5), the fall of Eve and Adam (3:6,7), the seeking God (3:8-13), the curse (3:14-20), the provision of covering (3:21), the expulsion from Eden (3:22-24). Chapter 4 records the first murder and the first civilization.

The third great fact is the Flood, which is dealt with in chapters 5 through 9. Lesser details include the genealogy of Noah (chapter 5), the building of the ark (chapter 6), the Flood (chapter 7), the return to the land (chapter 8), and the covenant with Noah (chapter 9).

The fourth great fact is the beginning of nations (chapters 10 and 11). This was brought about by the confusion of tongues as a result of God's judgment at Babel.

The fifth great fact is the call of Abraham. The Holy Spirit uses chapters 12 to 25 to record events relating to the life of Abraham. Again there is the list of lesser details, from the time of his call (12:1-3) to his death (25:7-10). Man had turned away from God. The Lord chose Abraham to father a chosen nation, Israel. From him came the lineage which provided the promised Redeemer. Of special note are the types of Christ and His redemption in these chapters—Melchizedek (14:18-20; compare Hebrews 7 and Psalm 110) and the substitute ram offered in Isaac's stead (22:13,14). The apostle Paul used Abraham as an illustration of justifying faith in Romans 4.

The biography of Isaac follows next (chapters 21-28). Isaac is noteworthy as a type of Christ—a type in his birth which was both supernatural and predicted and a type in his sacrifice when offered by his father as an only son. His return from the place of sacrifice was a type of Christ's resurrection. The incidents surrounding his marriage to Rebekah offer several beautiful pictures of Christ and His Bride.

The seventh major fact of Genesis is the history of Jacob (chapters 25-36). Major lessons to be learned from the life of Jacob are: (1) the grace of God as manifested on behalf of Jacob; (2) the illustration of prevailing prayer at Peniel; (3) God's estimate of faith, for Jacob received the Lord's blessing because of his appreciation of spiritual things; (4) when Laban cheated Jacob it bore out the principle of reaping what is sown.

The last biography is that of Joseph to whom God saw fit to devote the greater part of 14 chapters of Genesis. As with Isaac, there are many types of Christ in the life of Joseph, such as: (1) his father's love for him (Genesis 37:3; John 5:20), (2) the hatred of his brothers (Genesis 37:8-27; Matthew 27:1,2,22,23); (3) his temptation (Genesis 39:7-20; Matthew 4:1-11); (4) his promotion by Pharaoh (Genesis 41:40-44; Mark 16:19); (5) his marrying a Gentile bride during his rejection by his brothers (Genesis 42:50; Acts 15:14); (6) his revelation of himself to his brothers (Genesis 45:3; Zechariah 12:10).

A brief recap will indicate the following outline of Genesis which will help one to think through the book.

Primeval
Chapters 1-11
(1) Creation (chapters 1,2)
(2) Fall (chapters 3,4)
(3) Flood (chapters 5-9)
(4) Nations (chapters 10,11)

Patriarchal
Chapters 12-50
(1) Abraham (chapters 12-25)
(2) Isaac (chapters 21-28)
(3) Jacob (chapters 25-36)
(4) Joseph (chapters 37-50)

6. How does Genesis, the book of beginnings, relate to the Bible's central theme?

____

____

____

____

How does Genesis relate to Exodus?

____

____

____

Now let's move to the New Testament for a survey of one of the Gospels. The writers of the four Gospels all presented Jesus, but each from a different viewpoint. None attempted a complete biography. They selected incidents and discourses to emphasize the particular message which met the needs of the people to whom they wrote. All wrote to all mankind but each wrote primarily for a particular group.

Which book are we going to study?

The Gospel of Matthew

Who is the human author of the book?

Once again the author is not stated in the book itself, but reference materials uphold that Matthew, one of the disciples, wrote this book.

Who were the original recipients of this book?

Matthew intended his message primarily for the Jews.

What is the occasion leading to and the date and place of the writing of the book?

The occasion leading to its writing was to present Jesus as He was revealed in His words to the Jewish community. The date of writing is estimated between the early 50s and late 70s A.D. It is suggested that Matthew's Gospel was written in Palestine, due to its Jewish nature, but many also think it may have been written in Syrian Antioch.

Read the book through several times to find some key words or expressions used by the author. List them with references.

The key idea is the word "fulfilled" or the phrase "that it might be fulfilled." Matthew makes at least 60 references to the Old Testament writings as fulfilled in Christ. See resource 6B, "Christ—The Fulfillment Of Prophecy," for a partial listing of references.

What are the purpose and theme of the book?

The purpose and the scope of the book are indicated in the first verse. As the son of David, Jesus is shown as King; as the son of Abraham, He is obedient unto death. Often repeated words are *kingdom, kingdom of heaven,* and *son of David.*

What are the key facts in the book? Use these to develop a brief outline.

Matthew's Gospel shows Christ through the Lord's speech, words, sayings, discourses, and doctrines. As Matthew writes, he refers to and unfolds the significance of the past. George Henderson, in *The Wonderful Word*, has given the following simple outline of Matthew's Gospel.

1. The Person Of The King: 1:1 through 4:16

   a. His relation to earth: true, but sinless man; chapters 1 and 2
   b. His relation to heaven: beloved of the Father; chapter 3
   c. His relation to hell: conqueror of the devil; chapter 4

2. The Preaching Of The King: 4:17 through 16:20

3. The Passion Of The King: 16:21 through 28:20

It's Your Turn

Select a book for study. One of the shorter New Testament Epistles as suggested previously might be a good choice to begin with. Follow the procedures presented in this study and the format provided to assist your survey. Additional reference books may be beneficial also.

✎ **7. Which book are you going to study?**

____

✎ **8. Who is the human author of the book?**

____

____

✎ **9. Who were the original recipients of the book?**

____

____

✎ **10. What is the occasion leading to and the date and place of the writing of the book?**

____

____

____

____

11. Read the book through several times to find some key words or expressions used by the author. List them with references.

12. What are the purpose and theme of the book?

13. What are the key facts in the book? Use these to develop a brief outline.

SUMMARY

When surveying a book of the Bible, read the book from beginning to end without observing the chapter and verse divisions. Read it through several times, without the aid of a commentary, to determine the flow of ideas or outline. Remember to read prayerfully, allowing the Holy Spirit to enhance your understanding of His message to you.

Taking a survey of a Bible book improves understanding of the unity and interrelationship of the whole Bible. As we read and reread the books of the Bible, we will begin to see the picture of each book and the overriding theme of the entire Bible. Taking a forward glance over the entire contents of the book to get a survey of all the content lays a foundation for further Bible study. But a Bible survey is meant to be more than an intellectual feast. If we approach the Bible with a proper attitude of prayer, we can expect to find great truths to enrich us spiritually, mentally, and physically.

LET'S REVIEW

1. What is meant by Bible synthesis?

2. Name the rules to follow in synthetic study.

3. What are the advantages of this type of Bible study?

4. What is the central theme of the Bible?

5. What is the purpose and the key word of Genesis?

6. How can you make this method of study a part of your personal Bible study program?

Study 7

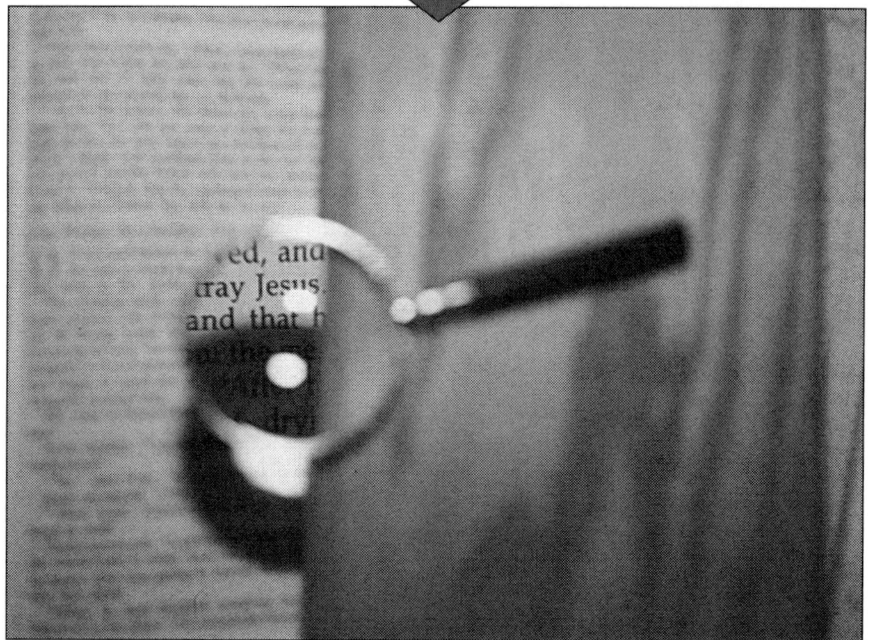

Taking A Closer Look

Bible study is a lifetime occupation. It is a task that is always unfinished. The more we read and study the inexhaustible riches of Bible truth, the more convinced we will be that no better investment of time can be made. The inductive method of Bible study will help us to analyze passages of the Bible to discover deeper truths.

In this method of Bible study, we carefully examine a particular passage of the Word of God for the purpose of understanding its content, meaning, and application. This involves observation, interpretation, and application, and requires analysis. At first we notice only what is obvious, but continued study will train us to discover deeper truths.

Bible analysis places emphasis on the thread of truth. This thread can be found in a book, a chapter, a paragraph, even a verse. Finding the thread points to the essential unity of the Bible.

Observation: Analyzing The Text

The Bible is unique among all the books of literature. It is a library, made up of 66 books, long and short, authored by about 40 men over a period of about 1,600 years. Despite its diverse authorship over this long period of time, it has a oneness or unity of message. This overall unity indicates the purposeful design of the Almighty, for the Word of God is like a skillfully constructed building.

In literature, form or structure of the text is important. This is the key to be used in unlocking the contents. Any literary work is constructed around one main structural framework. Study reveals that the basic structure is made up of smaller units of composition. These are seen to be related to each other and to the whole.

From a literary standpoint, the Bible stands alone, above all literary classics. Within its books, we will find biography, history, poetry, narratives, law, parables, dialogue, and prophecy. It is important for us to be aware of the literary form of the book or passage we are investigating. If it is dialogue, who is speaking, what is he saying, and for what group is the message intended?

Observation cannot yield maximum information if the student doesn't know that the form is important. The Holy Spirit moved upon men of old to write words in the structural framework of the Bible which are meaningful in contributing to the whole. In other words, the writers did not record unrelated and aimless words. All that was said was inspired of God and was written with purpose. Each literary form yields truth in its own unique manner. Those who are aware of this and seek to broaden the scope of their understanding in this area will benefit in many ways.

The Holy Spirit directed each writer of Scripture to record only those things which needed to be said on a given subject. Seldom, if ever, was everything included that could be said on a matter, whether it was a discourse, a biography, or historical record. The Bible is not and does not claim to be a record of history, a text on science, or a code of ethics. Instead, the authors were inspired to select those things which would accomplish the purpose of their books. The material selected was arranged to suit that purpose.

To analyze or examine a given passage properly, and to understand the intent and meaning of the author, we must pay attention to the content and form of the passage. All God authors has order, form, and purpose. It is not enough to study some parts and bypass others.

We must let the Bible speak for itself. In our quest to know God's truth, as revealed in the Scriptures, we ask: "What does God say?" and, "How does He say it?" We must observe the usage of terms and determine which are literal and which are figurative.

Every passage of Scripture contains a principal truth. In addition to the primary meaning, there often is a truth which is less obvious. A certain truth in a given passage may be very evident while, on the other hand, there could be a less apparent gem to be dug out. We have the task of ascertaining what the Holy Spirit intended to say.

So how do we determine the true meaning of a passage? What is literal? What is symbolic? Before we can correctly interpret a portion of Scripture, we must correctly observe these features.

Diligent application of four steps is required to observe Scripture properly: (1) read and record; (2) search; (3) relate; (4) recall.

Read And Record

Bible study begins and ends with reading. Paul highlights this in 1 Timothy 4:13 when he urges Timothy to commit himself to the public reading of the Scriptures.

It is advisable to make notes when studying. Record observations, no matter how insignificant they may seem at the time, so you will be able to recall through meditation what the Holy Spirit has made real to you. Someone once said that a pencil is the third eye for seeing scriptural truth. The other two are the eye of the Holy Spirit and the physical eye. To study with pencil and notebook at hand cultivates the powers of observation, orderly thought, and memory.

1. What does Proverbs 12:27 say about the diligent man?

____

____

How should we relate this to our study of the Scriptures?

____

____

____

Search

The Holy Spirit has caused Scripture to be recorded in a manner to challenge us. The secrets of the Word are as "silver" and "hid treasures" which are to be sought after (Proverbs 2:4). Sanctified effort is needed for this searching of the Word.

2. Read 1 Corinthians 2:9-12. What do these verses reveal about the assistance available through the Holy Spirit during Bible study?

____

____

____

Relate

A next step in finding the meaning of a passage is to relate it to other passages. The Bible does not contradict itself. Truth is many-sided. Both Paul and James draw their respective arguments regarding faith and works from the same Old Testament patriarch—Abraham. Paul writes of obedience in faith (Romans 4) and James writes of obedience in action (James 2:21-24). They deal with complementary aspects of one truth. Analyzing the passages separately is very enlightening, but a new appreciation of the total subject of faith and works is gained as we compare the passages and observe the relationships. The better things of Christ, as recorded in the Epistle to the Hebrews (Hebrews 8:1 to 10:18), take on enriched meaning as we become acquainted with the tabernacle of Moses and the Old Testament offerings.

3. List the relationship between faith and action mentioned in each verse below.

Matthew 9:22 ______________________________

____

Romans 4:18-22 ______________________________

____

Romans 5:1 ______________________________

____

Recall

So far these steps of observation have required concentration and effort. The next requires something else—meditation. The word *meditate* is from a Greek word meaning "to attend." To meditate is to give attention, to ponder prayerfully. This is what we are admonished to do in Proverbs 2:1-3.

The record we keep of all our observations is important. Whether or not the items which occur to us seem important or not, record them. The noting of small items, seemingly insignificant at the time, may become more prominent as we begin to sift through our observations.

We need to note the following: (1) points; (2) problems (What does this passage say that I don't understand?); (3) parallels (What similar truths are found elsewhere in the Bible?); (4) precepts to obey; (5) promises to claim; (6) dangers to avoid.

G. Campbell Morgan outlined four rules for this kind of study. He said, "Read and gain an impression. Think and gain an outline. Meditate and gain an analysis. Sweat and gain an understanding."

Interpretation: Letting The Text Speak To You

To know what the author says puts us well on the way to understanding what was meant. Correct observation is necessary for correct interpretation.

A passage may have only one interpretation but several applications. In 1 Corinthians 10:1-11, Paul makes an application of the things that happened to the Children of Israel during their wanderings in the wilderness.

4. List at least 3 practical applications for each of the principles taught in the following passages:

Philippians 1:21 ______________________________

____

____

Ephesians 6:5-9 ____________________

____

____

1 Thessalonians 5:26 ____________________

____

____

We should determine the meaning of a passage, not verify our prejudices or traditions. Martin Luther advised that effort should be made to find the meaning of a passage, not import one into it. It is wrong to use verses as hooks upon which to hang doctrinal beliefs. Passing references are not to be used for establishing doctrine.

Not all Scripture is easily understood. We may even grasp a Bible truth and yet never understand all of the implications of that truth. One of the enriching experiences of Bible study is the constant discovery of these truths. We will never exhaust the great riches of Bible content this side of eternity. The biblical authors even recognized some things were not for their immediate understanding when they found a passage to be totally beyond their comprehension.

5. How is the depth of God's wisdom expressed in the following verses?

Deuteronomy 29:29 ____________________

____

Job 12:13 ____________________

____

____

Isaiah 40:13,14 ____________________

____

Isaiah 55:8,9 ____________________

____

____

When two interpretations can be proposed for a given passage, the clearest should be accepted. The clear passage should interpret the obscure; not the obscure, the clear.

Essential truth is not veiled by obscure and incidental passages. Essentials are not hidden mysteries. Everything necessary to salvation and Christian living is set forth clearly.

6. John 3:16 provides a clear declaration of essential spiritual truth. List the 4 principles of salvation presented in John 3:16.

____

____

____

APPLICATION: APPLYING THE BIBLE TO EVERYDAY LIFE

Application is the ultimate purpose of Bible study. We may know what God says and how He says it, we may know what the Bible says and what it means, but it only becomes of personal value when we make a personal application.

7. What does James 1:22-25 teach us about the value of applying God's Word to our lives?

____

____

____

We might ask ourselves the following questions to make our study relevant to our lives:

1. What does the Bible say (content)?
2. What does the Bible say to me (personal application)?
3. What does the Bible say to me today (relevant personal application)?
4. What am I going to do about it today (immediate personal action on God's Word to me)?

Our will is central to making Bible study relevant to life. We must choose to study and as we study we must choose to obey. If we do not take in and make Bible truth a part of our lives, spiritual atrophy will result.

8. What promises does Jesus share regarding those who do apply the words of God?

Mark 4:23-25 ____

____

Luke 6:46-49 ____

____

____

What will be the result of lack of application?

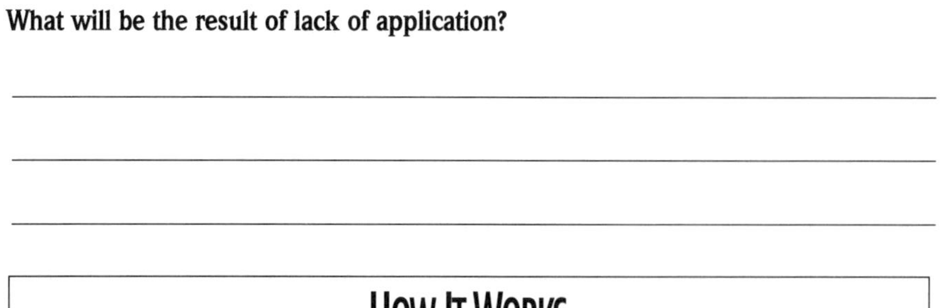

HOW IT WORKS

We are now ready to examine a portion of Scripture. Let's make a brief recap of some practical suggestions.

Approach your study time with freshness of mind. Your best study is not done when you are weary mentally and physically.

Choose the passage. Read it over several times. Get an overview of the whole, then explore the parts. Try to arrive at the intentions of the author. Find the purpose and note key words and expressions. What is each paragraph or unit of thought trying to say? Do paragraphs differ? How? What seems to be the thread of unity throughout? Search for this thread or chain. Connect the links of the chain.

Keep a record of all your observations, whether you think they are significant or not. After you have noted the words or phrases which seem to reflect the author's purpose and have found the thread of thought, you are ready to search for outside help on problem passages, look at parallel passages, and compare geography, history, and the like.

Through the entire process, it is of utmost importance to depend upon the Holy Spirit without whom we cannot understand the Word of God.

Ephesians 1:3-14 contains a volume of truths and doctrines vital to Christian faith and practice. Let's apply the study principles we have discovered.

What passage of Scripture have we selected?

Ephesians 1:3-14

What key words and expressions are prevalent?

The expressions "in Christ" and "in Him" are found throughout this passage.

What is the purpose for the writing of this passage?

These verses combine into a great hymn of triumphant praise to God. They describe the work of the Triune Godhead in salvation.

What is each unit of thought trying to say?

God the Father planned redemption for us. In tribute to the Father (verses 3-6) three of His acts on our behalf are mentioned: He chose us (verse 4); He adopted us (verse 5); He accepted us (verse 6). Acceptance is through the work and merit of the Beloved, His only begotten Son.

God the Son provided salvation for us. Verses 7-12 pay tribute to the work of Christ. He redeemed us (verse 7); He has made known the mystery of His will (verse 9); He has made us heirs (verse 11).

God the Holy Spirit has wrought salvation for us. He has given us: a seal (verse 13); a deposit of our inheritance (verse 14); a pledge of that perfect redemption that will be ours at Christ's coming (verse 14).

Each of the three tributes to the Trinity ends with an expression giving praise to His glory (verses 6,12,14). All God's purposes center in himself and are for His glory.

What seems to be the thread of unity throughout? Connect the links in the chain.

God's majestic plan of salvation from before time (verse 4) to beyond time (verse 10).

What parallel passages did we find to support our findings?

John 3:16; Exodus 15:2; Jonah 2:9; Luke 1:67-79; Hebrew 2:3,4

What life application can we make from this passage?

Each Person of the Trinity is and always has been personally interested and involved in providing a way for our salvation. What a gift!

IT'S YOUR TURN

Select a passage of Scripture you would like to explore for deeper meaning. Follow the procedures just illustrated using the format provided to assist you.

9. What passage of Scripture have you selected?

____

____

10. What key words and expressions are prevalent?

____

____

____

11. What is the purpose for the writing of this passage?

____

____

____

____

12. What is each unit of thought trying to say?

13. What seems to be the thread of unity throughout? Connect the links in the chain.

14. What parallel passages did you find to support your findings?

15. What life application can you make from this passage?

SUMMARY

Martin Luther said he studied the Bible in the way he gathered apples. He would first shake the whole tree so the ripest apples would fall. This he compared to study of the Bible as a whole. Next he would climb the tree and shake each limb, comparable to a survey of each book of the Bible. Then he would shake the branches, similar to chapter study. Next he would shake each twig, a picture of paragraph and sentence or verse study. Last, he would look under each leaf, comparing this to word study.

Bible study should be considered a continuous process. By it we learn and grow. As we carefully and prayerfully read the Bible, the Holy Spirit will help us see ways to apply it to our lives. As we apply it, God will continue to bless us with understanding.

LET'S REVIEW

1. What is meant by *inductive* study? Compare it to synthetic study.

2. What is meant by *observation*? *interpretation*? *application*?

3. Why doesn't the Bible give a complete record of historical events?

4. What is the function of the Holy Spirit in Bible study?

5. What will be the benefit of including the inductive method of study in your overall Bible study plan?

Study 8

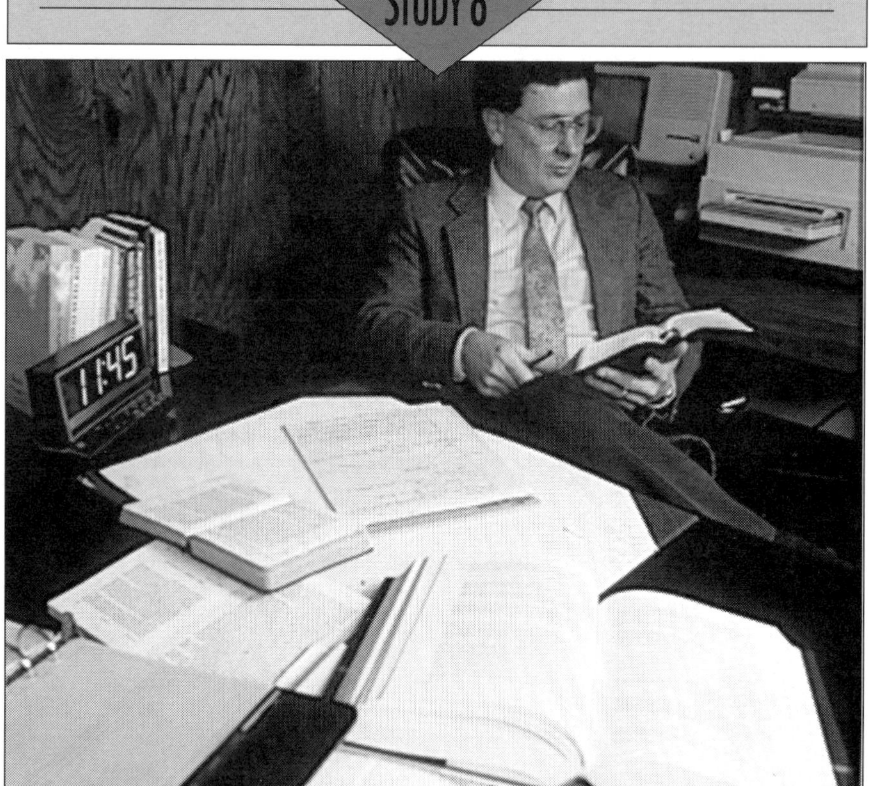

Studying The Bible Topically

Topical study is considered one of the most popular types of Bible study. With the use of a good concordance, this type of study approach becomes one of the easier methods. This method is different from other Bible study methods because the subject is the starting point instead of a passage of Scripture. Bible verses that relate to the chosen subject are then found.

A topical study of Christian doctrine is an important part of Bible study. Doctrinal truth is found in all the Bible. The more we study, the more we are amazed with the range of revealed truth. The study of doctrine is not reserved for theologians. Every Christian should study doctrine, for the entire structure of Christianity rests upon this foundation.

The Value Of Studying Topically

Study by topics will equip a person with a fundamental understanding of the great doctrines and principles of the Bible. Teaching a doctrine with only a few selected texts is dangerous and can lead to error. When we gain proper emphasis and understanding of all the Bible teaches on a given topic, we will be kept from error and grounded in the truth.

Millions of people listen when the leaders of their country outline programs or make announcements affecting their welfare. It is far more important to hear what God has to say on great subjects which have a bearing on them for all time and eternity. Too many people know a part of what God has to say—usually only a small part—and so their knowledge is incomplete and their ideas are imperfect. They can only know what God has to say on any topic by going through the Bible and gathering information on what He has said.

Some people will only accept truth which a church recognizes. They accept the dogma of a church over the doctrines of the Bible.

1. Using a standard dictionary, define the term *dogma*.

____

Others will accept no truth other than what natural human intellect can reason out. Still another group looks to visions, dreams, and operations of the gifts of the Holy Spirit for spiritual direction.

There is, however, only one source for doctrine, the only truly sufficient rule book for faith and practice. That is the Bible. As the Supreme Court is the final court of appeal for legal problems in the United States, the Bible is the final authority for Christians. Dogmas, human reasonings, and supernatural manifestations are correct only as long as they agree with the Word of God.

2. According to Ephesians 4:14, what is the purpose of establishing a firm foundation of biblical doctrine?

____

____

Two words translated "doctrine" occur some 50 times in the New Testament. These two Greek words, *didache* and *didaskalia*, bear the meaning "teaching, the work of a teacher, and the thing taught." *Doctrine* means "teaching" or "instruction" and can be either good or bad. There are true doctrines and false doctrines.

3. What does the Bible teach concerning the Christian's need to understand doctrine?

Titus 2:7,8 _______________________________________

1 Timothy 4:6 _____________________________________

2 Timothy 4:2-5 ___________________________________

Titus 1:13 ____________________

1 Timothy 6:3,4 ____________________

2 Timothy 1:13 ____________________

An important subject classified under topical study is Christian doctrine, therefore we emphasize this vital subject. We need not be greatly concerned about creeds and dogmas, but we must be concerned about doctrine which is the foundation of Christ's Church. Heresies would not gain such large followings if believers were rooted and grounded in Christian faith.

Myer Pearlman (an early Pentecostal pioneer) stated, "Strong beliefs make for strong character; clear-cut beliefs make for clear-cut character. Of course, a person's doctrinal belief is not his religion any more than the backbone is the man's personality. But as a good backbone is an essential part of a man's body, so a definite system of belief is an essential part of a man's religion."

We must guard against studying only those topics that appeal to us. There is a tendency with most of us to do those things which are of special interest to us. Many of us tend to overemphasize certain truths, or rather, fail to give proper emphasis to other areas of truth. To be physically healthy we must maintain a balanced diet. In like manner, we need a balanced spiritual diet by feeding on all the Word of God.

4. What would be the danger of focusing on the study of prophecy but failing to have an interest in the basic principles of daily Christian living?

____

____

Most of us can think of people who have made a nuisance of themselves because they are fixated on a few pet subjects. They are lopsided, for though they are well-informed on their favorite topic, they are uninformed on many subjects equally important.

To avoid a lack of balance, we should make topical study systematic. It should be comprehensive and cover more than just a casual treatment of the topic. Try to use as many Scripture references as possible.

Avoid the temptation of attempting to determine what the Bible says about a topic before you actually study it. Likewise, don't attempt to use the Bible as a tool to ratify your personal beliefs.

How To Study Topically

Topics of the Bible generally fall under the following classifications: (1) doctrines; (2) events; (3) places; (4) duties; (5) words; (6) biographies.

After choosing the topic to be studied, list all the passages that relate to the subject. Be thorough at this point. Find all the Bible has to say on it. A good concordance, a topical textbook, and margin references will be very helpful. The followers of the cults err at this point. They are usually very free in quoting the Bible to prove their point, but they use isolated or selected texts without proper consideration for all the Bible has to say on the matter.

We must be exact, as well as thorough. Determine the exact meaning of the passage with regard to the topic under study. Observe before seeking to interpret. Study the meaning and usage of words.

A Bible dictionary and margin translations are very helpful. Various translations should also be used for comparison. Examine passages in the light of parallel passages and words in comparison to parallel words. A study of context, parallels, and word meanings will usually clarify the meaning of a verse when it appears difficult. The meaning of many of the difficult passages in the Scriptures is made plain by other passages.

After noting all the Bible has to say on a subject and recording it on paper, the next task is to arrange the results. Usually we will have accumulated a large amount of material. Now we must organize it. The mere accumulation of many verses for the sake of being comprehensive is not enough. Verses should be chosen to make the subject clear and easily understood. The result should be an analysis, combining sufficiency of details with clarity of meaning.

Always bear in mind the need for the help of the Holy Spirit. Those who have never known the touch of the Spirit are not certain that truth, real and complete, can be found. As the centuries have passed, one system of philosophy has followed another. Searchers after truth have found human systems to be incomplete and unsatisfying. But Jesus did not say truth would come by human searching and human intellect alone. Neither did He say that truth in its fullness would come in a moment.

5. What promises did Jesus make concerning our understanding of the Bible's truth?

John 8:31,32 ____________________

John 16:13 ____________________

Application of what we have learned on the subject under study must be made. The object of our study is not attained until the truth is applied in a manner to create a response. Bible truth must be translated into Christian living.

HOW IT WORKS

Let's apply the procedures just presented to study the subject of prayer.

What doctrine or term are we going to study?

Prayer

How many times does the term or a close relative of the term appear in the Bible?

• Pray occurs	292
• Prayed occurs	65
• Prayer occurs	114
• Prayers occurs	24
• Prays occurs	9
• Praying occurs	20
Total	524

How many times does it appear in the Old Testament vs. the New Testament?

	OT	NT
• Pray occurs	225	67
• Prayed occurs	31	34
• Prayer occurs	83	31
• Prayers occurs	2	22
• Prays occurs	4	5
• Praying occurs	6	14
Total	351	173

How does the Bible define the term?

- Communion (1 John 1:3; 2 Corinthians 3:18)
- Appeal (Ephesians 6:18; Philippians 4:6)
- Intercession (Romans 8:26,27)
- Consisting of adoration, thanksgiving (Philippians 4:6), confession (James 5:16; 1 John 1:9), petition (1 John 5:15)

Arrange the passages into categories.

A. Prayer is described as:

- Calling on the Lord (Genesis 12:8)
- Pleading with the Lord (Exodus 32:11)
- Pouring out one's soul (1 Samuel 1:15)
- Crying to heaven (2 Chronicles 32:20)
- Seeking God (Job 8:5)
- Making petition (Job 8:5; Jeremiah 36:7)
- Looking up (Psalm 5:3)
- Lifting up one's soul (Psalm 25:1)
- Crying to God (Psalms 27:7 through 34:6)
- Seeking the Lord (Psalm 27:8)
- Pouring out one's heart (Psalm 62:8)
- Drawing near God (Psalm 73:28; Hebrews 10:22)
- Lifting up one's heart (Lamentations 3:41)

B. Prayer is to be made:

- To God (Psalm 5:2)
- In the name of Jesus (John 14:13,14; 16:23,24)
- By the Holy Spirit (Romans 8:26,27)
- At all times
    - Night and day (1 Timothy 5:5)
    - Without ceasing (1 Thessalonians 5:17)
    - Always (2 Thessalonians 1:11)
    - Faithfully (Romans 12:12)
- Everywhere (1 Timothy 2:8)
- Without hypocrisy and egotistical repetition (Matthew 6:5-7)
- Fervently (James 5:16; Colossians 4:12)
- In faith (Hebrews 11:1,6; 1 John 5:14,15; Matthew 21:22; James 1:6; Hebrews 10:22)
- With submission to God (Luke 22:42)

C. Posture in prayer

- Standing (1 Kings 8:22; Mark 11:25)
- Bowing down (Psalm 95:6)
- Kneeling (2 Chronicles 6:13; Psalm 95:6; Luke 22:41; Acts 20:36)
- Falling on one's face (Numbers 16:22; Joshua 5:14; 1 Chronicles 21:16; Matthew 26:39)
- Spreading one's hands (Isaiah 1:15; 2 Chronicles 6:13)
- Lifting up one's hands (Psalm 28:2; Lamentations 2:19; 1 Timothy 2:8)

D. Answers to prayer granted

- Immediately (Isaiah 65:24; Daniel 9:21-23)
- Delayed (Luke 18:7)
- Differently from our desires (2 Corinthians 12:8,9)
- Beyond our expectation (Jeremiah 33:3; Ephesians 3:20)

E. Answers denied to those who

- Regard iniquity in their heart (Psalm 66:18)
- Live in sin (Isaiah 59:2; John 9:31)
- Ask incorrectly (James 4:3)
- Are hesitant (James 1:6,7)
- Are self-righteous (Luke 18:10-14)

Summarize discoveries in brief statements.

- Prayer, mentioned over 500 times in the Bible, is very important.
- Prayer is made to the Father in the name of Jesus.
- Prayer implies the existence of God and the responsibility of man, and has no meaning for those who deny either. It is more natural that God in His great mercy should answer the prayers of His children, than that earthly parents should grant the requests of their children (Matthew 7:11).

How can we apply what we have learned to our personal lives?

We should approach God with an attitude of worship, a sense of need, an assurance of faith, and submission to His will. We need to draw near to God in prayer, placing ourselves at His disposal, so He might channel His creative faith through us.

IT'S YOUR TURN

Select a doctrine or term of personal interest from the Bible. Follow the procedures just illustrated to complete your study. Use the format provided to assist you.

6. What doctrine or term are you going to study?

____

____

7. How many times does the term or a close relative of the term appear in the Bible?

8. How many times does it appear in the Old Testament vs. the New Testament?

9. How does the Bible define the term?

10. Arrange the passages into categories.

11. Summarize your discoveries in brief statements.

12. How can you apply what you have learned to your personal life?

SUMMARY

The topical method of Bible study can be very productive when it is used wisely. Its simple procedures, and the multitude of helps available, allow us to analyze what the Bible has to say about a volume of issues. We can gather passages to help us find biblical answers to situations as they arise in our lives, as well as investigate biblical doctrines. It is important to remember to consider all passages related to a subject, organize them, and analyze them before we draw conclusions and make applications. With the help of the Holy Spirit, God's Word will come alive to us through careful topical study.

LET'S REVIEW

1. What are the advantages of topical study?

2. List errors to avoid in topical study.

3. What is meant by *doctrine?* Why is its study important?

4. What tools aid in topical study?

5. List five topics you would like to study in the coming weeks.

Study 9

Studying Biblical Characters

Human life is one of the most fascinating subjects we can study. It is the human element that has appeal in every work of art, in every news story, in every event of daily life. Abstract principles take on meaning as they relate to life and find expression in the thoughts and actions of people. Ideals must come down to earth and walk in the guise of men to become useful and reasonable. The study of the lives of great men and women has always been a source of inspiration and help to succeeding generations.

The Bible is a book filled with fascinating biographies. God has chosen to give much of His Word in biographical form with divine purpose. He has used a method that captures our interest. When we live with Bible characters in their environments, their lives become meaningful to us. The narratives are rich in devotional lessons, applicable in everyday life. Basic principles are clearly set forth in a divine-human relationship.

THE VALUE OF BIBLICAL CHARACTERS

In proportion to its size, no book offers so large a collection of literature in which so many different persons appear as does the Bible. There are 2,930 separate persons mentioned in the Bible. Many of these are only mentioned by name, but hundreds of them furnish material for biographical study.

A biography can be described as a word picture of outstanding men and women. Is it any wonder that study of biblical characters is the most common method used in teaching children? How many of us did not become excited when we heard the stories of Bible people in our childhood? Just because we have become adults doesn't mean we still can't benefit from biographical studies.

Since God chose to use biography so extensively, and since all that He does has purpose, these biographies have meaning for us. The saga of human friendship is sung in the story of David and Jonathan. The love of husband and wife is beautifully portrayed by Jacob and Rachel. There are many pictures of home life—the hospitable home of Mary, Martha, and Lazarus in Bethany; the widow of Nain and her son. The frailties of man are portrayed—Judas the traitor, Peter who lost his head in a crisis, Balaam the prophet who was false for greed or gain. Knowledge of the persons of the Bible is necessary if we are to understand the Bible. It is both a privilege and a duty for us to make a study of Bible biographies.

1. What does 1 Corinthians 10:11 tell us about the stories of the people recorded in the Bible?

____

____

The characters pictured in the Bible graphically portray the story of the heart of man. All types are represented. They are not so idealized that they become irrelevant to life in their times or the problems of life situations in our day. The Bible sets forth people of like human clay. They are not flawless saints.

2. How is Elijah described in James 5:17?

____

____

God does not hide the fact that many of the greatest men of the Bible were guilty of folly and sin. The story is often recorded very frankly. Some of these men ascended to great heights of devotion and service, but at other times they fell into the depths of sin. God does not cover up for His people. He presents men who knew human struggle and failure.

David is a representative illustration. It is said of him that he was a man after God's own heart. Yet on occasion David was a liar, an adulterer, and a murderer. This does not mean that God condones sin. David was a man after God's own heart in that he repented of his sin and found God's pardon. The frailty of Bible men does not give us license to sin. These men were for types and examples, and their story is written for our admonition.

There is no glossing over the weaknesses or sins of the great and the good. The Bible records the duplicity of Abraham the upright man, the anger of Moses the meek man, the weakness of Samson the powerful man, the fear of Elijah the bold man, the carnality of David the devoted man, the folly of Solomon the wise man, and the failure of Peter the rocklike man.

The records of men are helpful because they are complete transparencies. Every portrait is faithfully realistic and instructive. Most paintings are of good men; some are of evil persons such as Absalom, Jezebel, Ahab, Naboth, and Judas. Good or bad, all are pictured objectively as warnings to us.

Bible biographies help to clear up moral and religious problems. Abstract discussions are of little help to men. But relate the matter to an expression of personal struggle and the picture changes. Take Jacob and Peter for example. Separate the moral and spiritual aspects of their character from their personal struggle, and it seems as so much theory. Relate their character to their personal problems and their lives are relevant to ours.

We must take into account God's true estimate of the men of the Bible. This will not lower these men in our thinking; rather, it will magnify the grace of God and encourage us. The biographies of the Bible have a spiritual value above all other biographies for they relate to us the reactions of the human nature to divine matters. From these lessons we learn how to avoid similar pitfalls and to better adjust our lives to the will of God and receive the great blessings of obedience to His will.

3. Read the following accounts of the life of Moses. What lessons can you learn from these experiences? Exodus 2:11-15; 3:1 through 4:31; 14:1-31; 15:1-21; 17:1-7; 33:1 through 34:35; Numbers 20:1-13

____

____

____

____

____

____

The study of Bible biographies has yet another value. God has chosen to reveal His plan and purpose through representative people. A knowledge of the people of the Bible is necessary if we are to understand the Bible. If we are to understand Genesis, the foundation book of the Bible, we must know and understand God's dealings with ten representative men—Adam, Cain, Abel, Seth, Enoch, Noah, Abraham, Isaac, Jacob, and Joseph.

Steps For Studying Biblical Characters

There are several principles, or guidelines, to follow when engaging in Bible study by biographies. The following list may prove too all-inclusive for some cases, but it will be a guide suggesting certain factors for which to watch.

As a first step, assemble all the references on the character to be studied. These references are often found scattered throughout the Bible. The bulk of the information may be found in one chapter or in a consecutive series of chapters. An isolated mention elsewhere in the Bible may contribute a great deal to our insight of the person's character. The New Testament has many enlightening statements which are clues to the importance of Old Testament persons.

Guard against confusing references relating to two or more persons having the same name. All persons must be accurately identified. To illustrate, there are six Marys mentioned in the New Testament.

4. Identify the Mary mentioned in each reference below.

Matthew 1:18 ____

Matthew 27:56 ____

John 11:1 ____

John 19:25 ____

Acts 12:12 ____

Romans 16:6 ____

There are four or five men named John, at least three named James, and eight who bear the name Judas. In the Old Testament there are 30 men by the name of Zechariah, 20 named Nathan, and 15 called Jonathan. The Bible lists only one Isaac, one Moses, one David, one Solomon, and one Isaiah. There is one Abraham and one Jacob, but the former was called Abram and the latter was renamed Israel. On the other hand, Peter had more than one name, being also called Simon, Cephas, and his surname was Bar-jona.

Determine the meaning of the person's name. Bible names are meaningful. They often express some significant characteristic. Jacob's name meaning "supplanter," was changed to Israel, meaning "a prince with God." God did this with purpose; it was not coincidence. It was at the point of his change of name that Jacob had a change of character.

Much can be learned by noting the background of the character under study. Trace the ancestry if possible. Did the character have an education, such as Moses or Paul, or did he/she come from a background such as Peter possessed? Where were the early years of the character spent? What were the influences of youth? Timothy, for instance, possessed a godly heritage, received from his grandmother Lois and mother Eunice.

A study of the friends and associates of characters will prove helpful. The friendship of David and Jonathan is an obvious example.

Take note of the places where the life story of the man unfolds. Oftentimes outstanding events in the lives of Bible men center around places of crises. Moses' life is in 3 divisions of 40 years each—40 years among royalty in Egypt, 40 years in Midian, and finally 40 years of leading the Israelites in the wilderness. Several of Paul's epistles become all the more meaningful when we realize they were written from a Roman prison.

5. What testimony about his life does Paul give in Philippians 4:11?

____

____

____

Observe particular traits of character displayed in various situations of the person's life. Paul, Peter, and John were strong leaders in the church. It is interesting to note how God used their particular traits to present His truths. Each sets forth one of the three cardinal graces of faith, hope, and love. Paul can be called the apostle of faith; his epistles are epistles of faith. In like manner, Peter is the apostle of hope as is revealed in his epistles. John, the beloved disciple, writes of love in his letters as the apostle of love. Jacob is another whose particular character traits shine through in the events of his life. And what of Peter with his impetuous spirit?

List the person's failures, faults, and shortcomings. What were the steps leading to failure? How did the failures affect the future?

Attempt to determine the great crisis in the life of the character. How did the person react?

Find the contributions made by the individual, contributions to that day and to ours.

What is the main lesson of the individual's life and what is its particular value to us?

How It Works

Now let's make a biographical study of Jacob according to the guidelines listed above. Jacob's life is particularly helpful as a character study. Many other Bible characters seem well nigh faultless. Men like Abraham, Joseph, Moses, Elijah, Elisha, Stephen, Paul, and John almost reach perfection. But Jacob was a man with faults. We are so much like him. The study of his life helps us to know that if God's grace and power can transform a deceiver such as Jacob into a prince having power with men and God, surely there is hope for us!

References

Space does not permit a listing of all Bible references to Jacob. He is mentioned 390 times, 366 times in the Old Testament, 24 in the New. A concordance would help here.

Meaning of name

Jacob means "supplanter" (Genesis 25:26). His name was changed to Israel, which means "a prince with God" (Genesis 32:28).

Ancestry

Jacob was the son of Isaac and grandson of Abraham who was the father of God's chosen people. Abraham, in turn, was a direct descendant of Noah through the line of Shem. Jacob and Esau were twin sons of Isaac and Rebekah.

6. What arrangement, contrary to natural tribal law, was spoken to Rebekah in Genesis 25:23?

____

____

7. What four events show a lack of confidence in God and of mutual respect between Isaac, Rebekah, and Jacob?

Genesis 25:29-34 ______________________________

Genesis 27:1-4 ______________________________

Genesis 27:5-13 ______________________________

Genesis 27:11-29 ______________________________

Friends and associates

Because of his deceit and trickery Jacob had to flee from home and friends. He found refuge with his uncle Laban. Here he served 14 years for the hand of Rachel. His wages were changed 10 times in 20 years.

Places of life experiences

Jacob's life unfolds in four places. He was a deceiver and supplanter in Beersheba, a servant in Haran still deceiving and being deceived, a saint in Hebron after his meeting with God at Peniel, and a seer in Egypt.

Traits of character

By nature Jacob was a supplanter. While he did wrong, at the same time he had set his heart on that which God had promised. He believed in the value of both the birthright and the blessing. He had an appreciation for spiritual values. While Jacob was shrewd, he was not bold. His approach to things was more that of a fox than of a lion. He slyly deceived; he fled from home rather than face Esau; and he slipped away without letting Laban know when he fled from him. But he was changed as we shall see.

Failures

Jacob tricked Esau out of his birthright (Genesis 25:27-34). He stole the blessing by deceiving Isaac (Genesis 27:1-33). He outwitted Laban with the cattle (Genesis 30:25-43). Jacob continued to deceive until transformed at Peniel. But he continued to reap for his wrongdoing. He lived as an exile and had a sad harvest of his evil years. There was the dishonor of his daughter Dinah (Genesis 34), the death of his beloved Rachel (Genesis 35:16-20), the supposed death of his favored son Joseph (Genesis 37), and the shame of his son Judah (Genesis 38).

Great crisis of life

Jacob's great crisis was at Peniel. Twenty years passed between Jacob's experience with God at Bethel and his experience at Peniel where he wrestled with God. When Jacob submitted, his name was changed to Israel, "a prince with God."

Contributions

Jacob contributed much to Israel and to us. His experiences vividly bear out what Paul wrote in Galatians 6:7—"a man reaps what he sows."

Lesson for us

God's blessings and prosperity do not always prove that all is right with a child of God. Jacob prospered when with Laban. God was gracious to him despite his deception. God commanded Jacob to return to the land of promise. There he would face Esau who had murder in his heart. It is an evidence of the faith of Jacob that he recognized God's voice and was willing to obey, even though as far as he knew, to submit to God's will was to risk his life and all that he possessed. Jacob had endured a long period of discipline in Haran, but the old nature still needed more change. At Peniel, God brought him to a conflict and crisis which became the great and final turning point of his life. Only after that was he able to face Esau and enter Canaan in the manner God wanted.

It's Your Turn

It's your turn to apply the principles just explained. Select a biblical character for your study. Use the format provided to assist you with your study.

8. Whom will you be studying?

____

____

9. References

____

____

____

____

____

____

10. Meaning of name

11. Ancestry

12. Friends and associates

13. Places of life experiences

14. Traits of character

15. Failures

16. Great crisis of life

17. Contributions

18. Lesson for us

SUMMARY

An examination of biblical characters is an exercise which results in spiritual strength. Those who study in this fashion will learn how God stretches individuals and shapes them into the people He wants them to be.

God continues to work His plan in His people today. Those who learn from the failures and successes of individuals who have gone before will find a smoother road to spiritual maturity.

LET'S REVIEW

1. How can the study of biblical characters help us grow in our Christian life?

2. Why doesn't the Bible gloss over the failures of great men?

3. Outline the 10 principles to follow in biographical study.

4. Why are names and places important in Bible study?

5. What lessons are to be learned from Jacob?

Study 10

Chapters, Verses, and Words

The original text of the Bible had no chapter and verse divisions. Chapters were introduced in about A.D. 1250 and verse divisions were made about 300 years later. Although not quite perfect as to units of thought, they are fairly satisfactory and are helpful to us in locating and identifying Scripture passages. For example, the theme of the well-known fifty-third chapter of Isaiah really begins with the last three verses of the preceding chapter.

The study of the Bible by chapter, verses, and words can bring rich rewards. There is a great difference between merely reading a chapter and reading it with understanding. The verses of the Bible are also significant, as are the words. We believe that every word in the original text was God-breathed. Never read so fast that the words are missed. Understanding of the meaning of a passage often depends on the understanding of a single word.

STUDYING BY CHAPTERS

To get the most benefit from chapter study, we should find an outline within the chapter. When we have established this, we can then begin to think our way through a book, chapter by chapter. There are several points to look for when studying a chapter of the Bible. They are: (1) main subject; (2) prominent persons; (3) key verses; (4) general information.

Main Subject

Most chapters of the Bible, in whole or in part, have a chain of development which emphasizes the main subject. It is a privilege to find this chain in a chapter. To find the chain, we observe the links.

A chapter must be read until an outline is discovered. You may not find even one great truth of a chapter on the first reading. The main subject and principal lesson becomes more obvious as you engage in prayerful reading and study. When studying, you should not leave a chapter until you have seen the development of some truth in it. If necessary, go ahead to the next chapter but come back to the chapter which is giving you difficulty. Every chapter has some spiritual teaching. Often the chapter that involves the most thought and at first refuses to yield its truths will, in the end, disclose a spiritual teaching of unusual richness.

1. Read Philemon. What is the main subject of this chapter?

____

____

____

Prominent Persons

Note the persons mentioned in the chapter. Pay attention to what is said about each one. Use a concordance to trace other references to those individuals. In the letter to Philemon, verse 23, Epaphras is mentioned as Paul's fellow prisoner. A check of your Bible's concordance will reveal two other references to him, both in Colossians (1:7; 4:12).

2. What do these other verses tell you about Epaphras? What was his relationship to Paul? List some key phrases and adjectives describing him.

____

____

____

____

____

Key Verse

Try to find the main verse, a key to the chain of truth in the chapter.

3. Determine the key verse in Philemon and write it below.

General Information

Find the commands to obey, the errors to avoid, the lessons to be learned, the promises to claim, and the prayers to use as patterns. How does the chapter relate to the great theme of the Bible, Christ and His redemption? How does it relate to the rest of the book?

4. What other important points did you find?

Make a note of words significantly recurring in the passage. Are there expressions peculiar to the chapter and to the book? Check the meaning of words you don't understand.

Summary

The above items indicate three general rules for chapter study: (1) relate the chapter to its context; (2) find the links in its chain of development; and (3) make personal application of the truths revealed.

5. What are the links in the development of this chapter?

6. What personal application can you make?

Studying By Verses

Some verses are historical in nature, others doctrinal, expository, narrative, or descriptive. Many Christians testify about the blessing received from a single Bible verse. Some of the richest truths and helps for Christian living are found in some single verse that stands out above all others in morning devotions. All day long the Holy Spirit uses it to strengthen the heart, inspire the life, fortify against temptation, and ignite for service.

If one verse is memorized each day for 6 days, then all reviewed on the seventh day, we would learn over 300 verses a year. When learning a verse meditate upon it; analyze it; take it apart and put it together again. Study the verse in relation to its context. Then find the chain of thought.

The key to the understanding of any sentence lies in understanding the verbs. The spiritual meaning rests on the exact force of the leading word or words. To understand the intent of the writer, we must ask what the sentence does or demands to be done.

7. Read Philemon 12-16. List all the verbs found in these verses.

____

____

What emotions of Paul are transmitted by the force of the verbs used?

____

____

How does the use of these verbs affect the reader?

____

____

Studying By Words

There is a wealth of meaning hidden in the words of the Bible. The more we study the Bible, the greater will be our interest in its words and their meanings. Every word in the original text is God-breathed. Correct understanding of the Bible comes through correct understanding of the words which the Scriptures use.

The delightful and profitable study of words enables us to see the remarkable variety, proportion, and balance of the truths of the Bible. For this kind of study we need a complete concordance which will include all references. For accuracy it is best, of course, to find the meaning of words by checking the original text. But even though we do not know the original Greek or Hebrew—and few of us do—we can do much with a good concordance. We should always keep our findings in a notebook so the results of the study can be referred to again.

8. Use a concordance or a Bible dictionary to find the name *Onesimus.* What does the name mean?

____

How would this information help you understand Paul's words found in verse 11?

____

____

____

Take a word and follow it through a book, or the books written by a certain author. Various authors use the same key word or words throughout many of their books. The word *precious* used by Peter in 1 and 2 Peter brings a rich outline of spiritual truth. Paul uses the key expression *in Christ* in his epistles. Romans presents justification *in Christ*; 1 Corinthians, enriched *in Christ*; 2 Corinthians, comforted *in Christ*; Galatians, liberty *in Christ*; Ephesians, fullness *in Christ*; Philippians, happy *in Christ*; Colossians, complete *in Christ*; 1 Thessalonians, caught up *in Christ*; 2 Thessalonians, hope *in Christ*.

9. Philemon is a very personal letter. Paul uses the terms *you* and *your* many times. Trace Paul's use of these words throughout the letter. What impact do these words have?

____

____

____

____

____

SUMMARY

The study of chapters, verses, and words is nearly inexhaustible. There are over 1,000 chapters, more than 30,000 verses, and hundreds of thousands of words. The study of each one will improve our comprehension of all of the Bible. Every word, or even letter, may be vitally important to the understanding of a passage of Scripture.

It is important to be exact when reading and quoting Scripture. The Bible is God-breathed and therefore demands careful attention to all that is in it. The Living Word is revealed through the words of the Bible. What a great way to get to know Jesus better!

Let's Review

1. When were chapter and verse divisions introduced to the Bible?

2. What should a person look for in a chapter to get a proper understanding and receive spiritual blessing?

3. What is the key to understanding a verse?

4. Why are Bible verses and words important?

5. How can verses and words become meaningful to us?

6. How can you use the study of chapters, verses, and words to enhance your Bible study?